D0810691

PARIS
REVIEW
EDITIONS

MEMORIES
OF
AMNESIA

MEMORIES

OF

AMNESIA

A Novel

LAWRENCE SHAINBERG

Paris Review Editions
British American Publishing, Ltd.

Portions of this novel appeared in slightly different versions in
The Paris Review

Copyright 1988 by Lawrence Shainberg
All rights reserved
including the right of reproduction
in whole or in part in any form
Published by Paris Review Editions/British American Publishing
3 Cornell Road
Latham, NY 12110
Manufactured in the United States of America

92 91 90 89 88 5 4 3 2 1

Library of Congress Cataloging in Publication Data

Shainberg, Lawrence, 1936–
Memories of amnesia.

I. Title
PS3569.H317M46 1988   813'.54   88-16647
ISBN 0-945167-00-8

FOR SUSAN

"I see nobody on the road," said Alice.

"I only wish I had such eyes," the King remarked in a fretful tone. "To be able to see Nobody! And at that distance too! Why, it's as much as I can do to see real people, by this light!"

—Lewis Carroll, ALICE IN WONDERLAND

Chapter One

Like so much brain damage, the first symptoms mine produced were almost indistinguishable from normal behavior. In a man less sensitive to his neurology they might have gone unnoticed; or if noticed, filed away among that enormous class of behavior (sometimes called, for want of a better word, *psychological*) one does not associate with the brain. For me, however, such dismissal was impossible. Twenty–one years a neurosurgeon, I had seen hundreds, even thousands of people with brain damage, and I knew all too well that the early symptoms were often so unremarkable as to leave no trace, even in brains unafflicted with amnesia, in the memory. Brain damage isn't always as grotesque as normal brains expect it to be. It's true that it can strike like a hurricane, but sometimes it's more like a gentle breeze, a subtle change of vectors that leaves you headed not in the opposite direction, but almost exactly where you were headed before. A charming eccentricity becomes obnoxious, private habits go public, it gets a little harder to keep things to yourself. I've seen it begin with farting or belching, nose-picking, cursing, bragging, talking or laughing too much or not at all, a lean to the left or a lean to the right, too many adjectives, self-absorption, visions of grandeur, arrogance, dogmatism, indecision or its opposite. In one patient the first symptom his tumor produced was an inability to admit mistakes. Another qualified everything he said. "It's only one man's opinion, but it seems to me that. . . ." There's nothing the brain can't use when it turns against you. Why should we be surprised that when it goes askew it proceeds at first along familiar routes, taking the line of least resistance, like water flowing down a mountain or an artist painting portraits of his friends?

At that time, I was operating on a young woman named Lucinda Roosevelt. She was conscious on the table, maybe that had something to do with it. It was only five years that I'd been doing this particular operation, and even though I was good at it—one of the best, to be frank about it—I'd never quite got used to it. When a patient is unconscious, his brain, as far as neurosurgeons are concerned, is flesh and nothing more. We build drapes around the incision so as not to see his face, avoid every thought of emotion, personality, etc. The reason is obvious: it's almost impossible to work with tissue if you grant it powers beyond itself. With conscious patients, patients like Lucinda, there's no way to hide from those powers, no way to deny that the cells you're invading are fundamentally the same as those that guide the invasion. Circularity, we call it, excessive reflection within the brain about the brain itself. You find yourself thinking that the tissue you're looking at is looking back at you. Nothing is more dangerous in a neurosurgeon, and as I see it, something in my brain found it, circularity, I mean, irresistible. In fact, ever since I'd begun performing this operation, I'd had the fantasy of performing it on myself, watching it all with mirrors, forcing my brain, in other words, to process images of itself. I don't agree with those who believe that fantasies of this sort, or circular thought in general, caused my distintegration (it's much more likely, in my opinion, that they were caused by it), but the fact that my neurology tended in this direction cannot be denied. The sad part is that my brain was never so quiet and focussed, so convinced of its own omnipotence as when engaged in speculation concerning, for example, the source within itself of the speculation in which it was engaged.

Lucinda was epileptic, her seizures so frequent and violent and uncontrollable that we had no alternative but surgery. She had to remain conscious because in seizure surgery the brain was mapped—using low-voltage electrical probes—and this required that she report on her responses. Only local anesthetic was administered. Her skull and scalp were deadened to counteract the pain of craniotomy, her brain (itself devoid of sensation) left free of all medication so as not to distort her perceptions. The idea was to locate the tissue that caused her seizures, defining its function so that we could excise it and cure her seizures. We had a rough idea of the target tissue, but before we could take it out we had to be precise about it, making sure not to

take too much, and to convince ourselves that she could
live without it—that we wouldn't leave her mute or
paralyzed or with some other dysfunction ranking higher
on the scale of neurological catastrophe than epileptic
seizures.

Twenty-four years old, Lucinda was an undersized
(pituitary dysfunction) black woman whose brain had
betrayed her on every level. Besides the seizures, her
pituitary problem, and a retardation that had left her
with the intellect of an eight-year-old, she was also
what we call an "idiot savante." Articles had been
written about her not only in scientific journals but also
in the popular press. Only recently, in fact, she had
appeared on a television special devoted to those with
her condition, demonstrating the useless memory skills
that allowed her to recall quantities of text or lengthy
mathematical equations or almost any other form of
linear information ingested by her brain. She didn't
understand what she was reading, but given a minute
to study a page of printed matter, she could recite it
years later, backward or forward. Filled with useless
information, her memory prevented her learning such
tasks as dressing herself or finding her way about the
house, but from what we could see, her incapacities—
like her seizures—did not disturb her. Despite her dysfunctions, she was gentle and charming and not without
a sense of humor. Almost everyone on our staff, myself
included, had grown more fond of her than we generally
liked to do with patients. I'd even found myself stopping
to see her when I wasn't making rounds. I enjoyed her

memory tricks and her malapropisms as if they were signs of intelligence and wisdom. Was this an early sign of my condition? I think so. I can't say that my problems began with Lucinda, but it seems to me that what I felt for her was a sign that my brain—long before its grosser symptoms made their appearance—had lost its capacity to limit its curiosity and keep me apart from that which aroused it. What could be more dangerous, for a man in my profession, than a breakdown of those particular neurological faculties that separate us from what we're supposed to study?

Diagnostic tests had determined that Lucinda's seizures originated in an area near the center of her Left Hemisphere. She had been positioned on her right side so as to turn her left side upward for surgical access. Her head rested on a thin black leather cushion and a system of clamps secured it, gripping it front and back with small foam-covered plates that my assistant, Eli Stone, had tightened with a pair of pliers. Altogether it took me nearly three hours to prepare her for mapping. The craniotomy was a large one, requiring an opening in her scalp and skull—what we called a "flap"—that stretched from the crown of her head backward toward her hairline, then forward on a line just above her ear to a point two centimeters in front of the ear, then upward on a slight diagonal to the crown of the head again. When I'd completed the superficial craniotomy and cut through and clamped apart the four layers of muscle and tissue that cover the brain, I placed my forceps on the instrument stand and with a quick sweep of my hand removed the drapes that had separated me from her face. Suddenly, Lucinda's left eye and ear and the left-hand corner of her mouth were visible below the opening I had carved in her skull. It was unclear whether she was smiling or whether the left side of her mouth had been drawn on an upward slant by the trauma to which she had just been subjected. Then too the disease that produced her seizures was located in cells not too far removed from those that controlled her mouth and cheeks. An inappropriate smile was one of her most common symptoms. "Hello, Sarah," I said. "Remember me?"

Lucinda's answer—a broader smile—made it clear that her first had not been inappropriate. Then again, even if it had been inappropriate, it would have remained, in all likelihood, an accurate indication of her mood. As I've noted, her condition was such that her spirits never sank. Along with the largest part of her intelligence, her pathology had eliminated, as far as we could discern, all sense of future time from the repertoire of her neurological functions. With no capacity for expectation she had none for fear or dread, and, except for moments of physical pain, no ostensible dissatisfaction with any circumstance in which she found herself.

Standing on my left, Eli nudged me with his elbow. " 'Lucinda,' " he whispered. "Name's 'Lucinda,' boss."

"Of course it's 'Lucinda.' Why are you telling me that?"

"You called her 'Sarah.' "

" 'Sarah'?" I could not deny that the name rang a bell. And once the bell was rung, others rang as well. That's the miracle of the brain. No bell rings alone. All at once the act of calling her "Sarah," unconscious until that moment, was everywhere I looked, a memory so clear I could not pretend I had invented it. What astonished me, however, was not my mistake but the fact that, as far as I was concerned, I had *chosen* it. The act of calling her "Sarah" had been anything but involuntary. This is why I say that this first symptom, the first, I mean, of my visible symptoms, was unremarkable to me. In fact, if anything was remarkable, it was the fact that the symptom did not disturb me. Knowing full well that "Lucinda" was her name, I had decided, with all my wits intact, to call her "Sarah"! The mistake was no mistake! This is not to say that it was normal but that *choice* was the symptom, not language. In other words, my problem was not in the cells that had *produced* "Sarah" but in those that had *made them do so*. What we often forget about brain damage is that it affects intention as well as behavior, wish as well as fulfillment. Sometimes it makes you do what you don't want to do, but just as often it makes you want to do what you shouldn't. Both conditions are grave, of course, but the odd thing that I discovered then was how much better a man can feel if he can locate his problem in the second category rather than the first. With all my experience, I certainly knew that dysfunctions of will are no less serious than dysfunctions of language, but once I concluded that I had chosen

"Sarah," my mistake became, not only insignificant, but just slightly, though I was far from ready to admit it, exhilarating.

During seizure surgery we used no respirator, so there was much less noise than during other procedures. The ceilings in the operating room were high and the walls of course very thick, so at times the room felt like a church or perhaps a spaceship, anything but ordinary time and space. When things were really quiet, the silence had a pulse that pounded like a drum. Except for that pounding, the only sound came from the instrument stand above the table, where a nurse named Ruth was rearranging the tools in preparation for stimulation. Overhead, the drumlights shown like the sun on a hazy summer day. I did not answer Eli. Not because I did not want to but because I'd forgotten what he'd asked. Instead I requested an instrument called a "rongeur" and made small adjustments at the edge of the flap, then adjusted the headlight strapped on my head, then turned my back to the table and studied Lucinda's x-rays, which were mounted on a light-box on the wall. Not one of these actions was necessary. My brain, like an army in retreat, was seeking positions where it could regroup. But signs of dysfunction proliferated. Twice in succession, I forgot what I was thinking about, and several disconnected phrases—"It seems to me," for example, and "Unless I'm mistaken" and (a happy sound) "No doubt about it!"—passed through my mind for no apparent reason. More disturbing, the urge to laugh aloud was often upon me, and I had begun to notice within myself feelings of exaltation. To see one's brain become dysfunctional is one thing, but to exult in that dysfunction is another. Only once or twice in my career had I seen patients who suffered from this syndrome— a need to celebrate their own disease, a belief that brain damage is a happy condition—but of all the nightmares the brain can produce, none is worse, and none—God, how well I knew this—is more difficult to treat. No physician can help a patient who rejoices in his disease. Even if you could locate, through the magic of brain-mapping, the cells that produce this type of distortion, what right have you to excise them when the patient himself does not desire it?

Sarah's vital signs were excellent. On the opposite wall an oscilloscope tracked her pulse and blood pressure, and electroencephalographic leads, taped to her skull, provided a constant display of her brain-wave pattern, which would be used to track epileptic activity, when and if it arose. Leaning close, I palpated her brain with a fingertip to get a rough sense of her intracranial pressure. For all her symptoms, it looked like any other brain. Oyster-grey with streaks of red and black, marked like a map by the lines of its convolutions, its surface rose and fell with her pulse like gently boiling water. An ordinary brain, as I say, but I stared at it as if I'd never seen one before. Naturally, the fact that it startled me so was startling in itself. Was it possible that the pathology I'd noticed earlier was focussed in the cells now engaged in processing this image? No one had to remind me that if the Optic Lobe lacks access to visual

memory it is sometimes incapable of distinguishing between the familiar and the unfamiliar. Of course, such
problems can be caused by memory alone, even if the
Optic Lobes are perfectly normal. Whatever the reason,
I could not avoid the suspicion that my memory was
impaired in some way, so much so that all the other
brains on which I'd operated were no longer available
to remind me, by comparison, that Lucinda's was not
extraordinary. Had I lost the habit that in the past had
ordered my perceptions? Was I about to enter, like so
many of my patients, a world devoid of history? A life
in which everything encountered would astonish me?
If so, why did I continue to feel exuberance and exhilaration? Had amnesia caused me to forget the horror
of such conditions, or had it caused me to invent such
horror when in fact it did not exist?

Far from distracting me, such questions passed me
by before I could pursue them. One of the pleasures of
brain damage is the way in which it interrupts the
normative relationship between questions and answers,
the freedom it grants one to ask questions without
concern for answers, or to delight in answers for which
no question is apparent. Disconnection of this sort, which
I was only now beginning to discover, was of course
the reason for my exhilaration, which—I know now—
was all the more intense because I could not understand
it. Nothing exemplifies neurological bondage like the
need for answers or the anxiety that follows questions
that do not produce them, and it was this bondage
which, without realizing it, I was beginning to escape.

The way in which my exhilaration increased when I could not answer the question, "Why am I exhilarated?"—that alone should have alerted me to the severity of my condition, but of course, if it had, my exhilaration might have diminished for the very reason it had increased. The resilience of the brain is never so apparent as in its ability to produce, from unanswered questions, answers to larger ones, and in this manner, to transform a position of weakness into one of even greater strength. Only reasoning as confused as that on which this paragraph is based will guard against such transformation and prevent the brain from accomplishing the miracle for which it is justly famous, snatching victory from the jaws of defeat or more precisely, illusions of clarity from illusions of incoherence.

I covered the flap with a towel and declared a short break before stimulation began. Orange juice was brought on a plastic tray, the straws extending from each cup bent so as to fit behind our operating masks, and we put some country music (Merle Haggard and Hank Williams) on the sterilized tape deck we kept in the instrument case. Except for the fact that voices were muted and nothing but eyes visible on our faces, our conversation might have taken place in the cafeteria. We spoke about a new Chinese restaurant that had opened near the hospital and a recent Swiss conference called "Neurology and Religion" where Eli, who was something of an authority on the subject, had delivered a paper called "Brain Wave Patterns in Experienced Meditators." He was a reasonable man, a first-rate neurosurgeon and a good researcher, but when it came to this sort of thing he was a bit excessive, to my mind, the kind of surgeon who liked to explain religious epiphany as neurochemical pathology. As far as he was concerned, people like Jesus and Buddha and Mohammed were neurological freaks whose inspiration had been produced by abnormal brain metabolism. He'd once published a paper, called "Brain Damage in Literature," which investigated the "symptoms" of characters like Ahab, Don Quixote, Molloy, and of course all the heroes of Faulkner and Dostoevsky. Fortunately, his greatest obsession wasn't neurology but food, so we barely skirted the conference before returning to the Chinese restaurant. Both Eli and the anesthetist, an old friend of mine named Harry Marks, had eaten there recently, and a ridiculous argument developed between them as to whether the place was worthy of their patronage.

Remembering that all of this was audible to Sarah, I was suddenly embarassed and not a little angry. Leaning forward, I addressed her in a whisper. Only after I had begun did I realize I had no idea what I meant to say. The words and phrases circulating earlier had assumed a higher volume and a dogged continuity. In effect, they were full-fledged voices now, the sort of thing my patients had told me about for years. They were beginning to nag me, interrupting my thoughts on the one hand, masquerading as them on the other. They were concrete sounds, muted but clearly external, like conversations on which I was eavesdropping. Sometimes they were coherent and sometimes not, sometimes impersonal and sometimes—as in the case of my father's voice, and my wife's—completely recognizable.

"No doubt about it!" I whispered.

"What?" said Sarah.

Clara Finch, the supervising nurse, came to my rescue. "What about you, Sarah? Do you like Chinese food?"

"What's Chinese food?"

"It's real spicy, with everything chopped up and covered with sauces."

Sarah thought it over for a minute. "I don't like nothing chopped up. I likes my food in little pieces."

"What Sarah likes," said Clara, "is Milky Ways. Isn't that right, sweetheart?"

A dreamy expression appeared on Sarah's face. "Oh Lord, yeah. Sometime a Snickers, but them Milky Ways—"

"What about Three Musketeers?" Eli said.

"I don't know no Three Musketeers."

"Baby Ruth?"

Sarah groaned. "Baby Ruth! I hate Baby Ruths!"

"Too bad for you," said Eli, who was deadly serious about his food. "Three Musketeers, in my opinion, is the only great candy bar made in America. I'm not talking about Swiss chocolate, mind you, but—"

Harry interrupted him. "Tell you what, Lucinda. You decide for yourself. Later, in the Recovery Room, I'll get you one from the machine."

"One what?"

"Three Musketeers."

"I told you—I likes Milky Way."

"You got it, sweetheart. To hell with Three Musketeers."

"She knows all the ingredients in Milky Ways," Clara said. "Isn't that right, Lucinda?"

"What's 'ingredients'?"

"What it's made of. What you read on the wrapper. Tell them what's on the Milky Way wrapper."

"Oh, that." Lucinda's eye—the one visible to us—rose in its socket until all but a tiny portion of the pupil had disappeared beneath the lid. Pausing as if to collect herself, she cleared her throat and licked her lips, and then, speaking in a monotone that sounded almost exactly like a computer, gave us what we had to believe was every word that could be found on the wrapper of a Milky Way. I don't remember all of it but I do recall, "Milk chocolate, corn syrup, sugar, milk, and partially hydrogenated vegetable oil," as well as the address of the company: "M&M Mars division of Mars, Inc., Hackettstown, New Jersey, 07840, U.S.A." Tell me, please, if it's more astonishing that her brain retained such information then than that mine should retain it now. Tell me how the brain decides what to offer us and what to withhold. Can any neurologist explain why I know the phone number of my high-school girlfriend? The entire pitching staff of the 1977 New York Yankees? "Hydrogenated vegetable oil"! "07840"! Who can measure the malice of an organ that generates such distraction? By what irony or fate did a few misdirected neurons determine that Lucinda, who could not remember her own mother's name, should remember "Hackettstown, New Jersey"?

I finished my orange juice and removed the towel that covered the flap. My moods and thoughts were shifting fast, almost equally divided between excitement and fear. One moment I felt disorganized, bereft; the next intrigued with these very sensations. The voices continued, my mother's especially, but they remained fragmentary and for the most part incomprehensible. Visible again, Lucinda's brain astonished me more than ever. The idea that the flesh at which I was gazing contained all the information on a Milky Way wrapper was alternately wondrous, infuriating, and a matter of indifference to me. In any case, my feelings for Sarah were very intense. Waves of affection, sadness, pity, and even, to my astonishment, envy. Yes, at moments it seemed she could teach me everything I needed to know, that she alone could protect me from the symptoms my brain had in store for me.

Father couldn't believe it. "What are you talking about? After all these years of treating brain-damaged patients, how can you be so romantic about the disease?" Naturally, I was embarassed. Twenty-one years a neurosurgeon, acting like a first-year medical student. Then mother reminded father how often tumors, aneurysms, epilepsy, etc. reveal themselves precisely in such romanticism, and my embarassment disappeared. Why? Because calling yourself romantic is a lot more upsetting than calling your brain romantic. Because it's easier to think of one's romanticism as a symptom than as a form of lazy thought or insufficient understanding. After all, a weakness of mind is embarassing, but a weakness of brain is simply a matter of fate. Even if it frightened me, it had no effect on my conscience.

"How's the EEG?" I said.

"Normal fluctuation," Harry said.

"Pressure?"

"One hundred over sixty."

"Okay, then let's get on with it." I lifted my hand toward the instrument stand. "Stimulator, please."

While I adjusted the electrode, Eli inserted the jack that linked it to the generator. We used a bipolar electrode, two platinum wires two millimeters apart, passed through a glass tube that served as a holder. The generator was a foot-controlled device that produced rectangular pulses .2 to .5 milliseconds in duration, one to five volts in strength. Nerve cells are good electrical conduits. Stimulation activates not only the cell touched by the electrode but also other cells along the same path, eventually reaching the end of that path to produce whatever behavior that particular circuit controls.

Mapping began, as usual, in the motor region, at the rear of the flap, just about the center of Lucinda's head. Even more than in other forms of neurosurgery, I had to keep my hand steady, so we used a bracing device, a sort of tripod that steadied my wrist. When a particular charge produced a particular response, a small label or ticket, as it was called, was placed in her brain at the point where the charge had been produced. We used different colors for different functions—white for motor behavior, blue for language, and orange for psychic affect. The logistics looked simple, but they required a great deal of cooperation among the staff. The labels, kept in sterilized containers on the instrument stand, were gripped with a tiny forceps and passed by Ruth to Eli who then placed them beneath the tip of the electrode, at the point that I'd just stimulated. Clara kept the operation's log, entering the ticket number and its corresponding behavior on the charts. Since that behavior was not always easy to define, it was often left for me to decide how to enter it on the chart, dictating aloud to Clara, as when the first ticket was installed: "White ticket number one: right thumb tremor."

The cells that controlled somatic function were situated, as I say, more or less in the center of the brain, describing a verticle line above Lucinda's ear. In this area, located at the rear of the flap, stimulations continued to produce unequivocal responses that could be transferred to the chart with almost no elaboration. Ascending from ticket #1, we developed movement and/or sensation in the index, then the middle, then the ring finger, etc. Tickets #6 through #11 produced tremors in the hand; #12, 13, and 14 in the wrist, elbow, and shoulder; #15 through 19 the hip, knee, ankle, and toes. Number 17 caused a jerk in the right leg, #19 a tickling sensation on the inside of the right calf. Moving down from the point that had caused the thumb-response, sensations were above the shoulders. Number 20 was in the neck, #21 the chin, #22 through #25 the cheeks and nostrils. Number 26 produced a twitch in the right eyebrow, #27 a fluttering of the right eyelid, and finally, #29 produced the same "inappropriate" smile we had seen so often on the ward.

I placed the electrode on the instrument stand, stepped back from the table and sang several bars of a song that had long been one of my favorites: "Oh Susannah!" Given the fact that I was known to be a bit eccentric, and that as chief of the department I was given wide berth in general with respect to my behavior, this did not elicit any comment from the staff. My pitch was too high and my voice too loud to be considered, as we say, "appropriate," but though eyes turned, no one except mother said a word, and she came to my defense.

"One hums or whistles to himself. What's wrong with singing?"

But I knew my voice had an independence it wasn't meant to have. As far as I could see, nothing in what I took to be my will, nothing of what I called "myself," had initiated this behavior. At this realization, a heady sense, very near to intoxication, came upon me. I felt as if I were embarking on a journey for which all my life had been a preparation. Even as I warned myself against such absurd conclusions, (reminding myself, as always, of patients who had presented similar delusions) I told myself that nothing before now had mattered, that nothing from now on would not.

Moving away from the Motor Region, we entered language tissue. We knew this because, at tickets #1 and #2, Lucinda's speech was slurred. We used blue tickets now, and photographs to test identification. At Labels #3, #4, and #5, we showed Lucinda, respectively, pictures of a woman, a tree, and an airplane, all of which she identified correctly. At label #5 she called a house "a horse," and at #6, a shoe produced an inarticulate stammer: "Sha-sho-sha-shapper." Stimulations #7–10 left her mute, with no response to the photographs, but at each of them, once the electrode was removed, she said, "I had it right, but I couldn't get it out." Sometimes we went back to a previous stimulation, and while the electrode was activated, asked her to count for us. At Labels #1–5, she did fine, but at #6–9 she had difficulty pronouncing numbers ("Three" was "throw," "six" "sags," etc.), and #10 through #14 produced a confusion of counting itself ("One, two, seven, nine, four . . .").

With motor and language-area sufficiently demarcated, and with no sign yet of epileptic activity, I knew that the pathological tissue for which we were searching would be found where we had expected, below a large convolution, the so-called "Fissure of Sylvius," in an area we called the "Interpretive Cortex." We used orange tickets there. Because cells in this area were not always, like those above them, specifically allied to function, the first five stimulations produced no dysfunction at all. The first "psychical" response occurred at orange ticket #7: "Oh, there's Mama!" Lucinda cried. "She comin' up the hill with the baby in her arms. Looka there! Uncle Jimmie behind her, and—"

She stopped because I had deactivated the electrode, thus interrupting the process through which the memory had been produced. Her voice was available of course, and words as well, but we knew from previous patients how quickly and completely such memories could be deleted from consciousness. Sometimes patients remembered what they'd seen even as they reported that they could no longer see it, and sometimes, as in Sarah's case, the electrode's removal produced an almost perfect void. I placed the electrode in the same spot and activated it again with the foot switch. Once again Lucinda saw her mother coming up the hill. The memory progressed from past to future like a film clip. She had a projector in her brain, no doubt about it, and I was turning it on and off with my foot. At Label #9 she found herself at the dinner table with her younger brother, and at Label #10–13, the electrode produced sensations she described as "spinning," "floating," or "flying."

For the first time, Harry Marks, watching the readouts from the electroencephalogram, noted that abnormal electrical activity in her brain was continuing after the electrode was deactivated. This first indication that the target area had been reached was supported by the fact that most of Lucinda's seizures began with sensations— spinning, flying, etc.—of the sort I had just produced. "Auras," they're called. Seizures like those from which Lucinda suffered—so called Psychomotor Seizures— could announce themselves with fear or anger, a distorted sense of time, changes in colors, dizziness, ringing in the ears, noxious odors, giddiness, a feeling of insects crawling on one's skin, or any of a hundred other sensations. An aura can be nothing more than a vague sense that something is wrong. Your home seems unfamiliar, or you feel at home in a stranger's house. No one understood the mechanism that initiated seizures, but there were as many triggers as auras: light flickering at a particular frequency, sound of a certain pitch, frustrating thought, painful memories, atmospheric conditions, emotions high or low, etc. Seizures could be hereditary, too, or caused by fevers or infections or birth injury or tumors or abcesses. But sometimes—we called this "Ideopathic Epilepsy"—they appeared for no reason at all.

What we did know, as a result of our surgical experience, was that stimulation of any brain could induce seizures, and therefore, that any brain could become epileptic if subjected to the right sort of irritation. That is to say, there is no brain so strong that certain cells within it cannot be induced to fire when they're not supposed to.

For the previous four months, Lucinda's seizures had lasted approximately ninety seconds and had occurred between ten and fifteen times a day. We couldn't be sure that all of them originated from a single source, but we had no doubt that a good deal of her problem emanated from the tissue we were stimulating now. Sometimes you can see signs of pathology around an epileptic focus—discoloration, for example, or a scar—but in Lucinda's case there was no visible difference between this tissue and that which surrounded it. Realizing that a seizure could come at any moment, I altered my pattern of stimulation, circling the region I thought most volatile. We didn't want our patients having seizures on the table, but we had to produce their auras to identify the tissue to be removed. I wanted a circle of labels if I could get it, a clear pattern to define the peripheries of the epileptic region. Ten of the next twelve stimulations produced after-discharge on the electroencephalogram, and eight of them produced auras such as dizziness and nausea and once—#9—a burst of laughter and the feeling she called "flying." Stimulation at tickets #15 and #16 produced not only the dizziness but also darting movements in the eyes, a dilation of the pupils, and slight tremors in the right hand. Number 17 and #20 caused her to laugh aloud and exclaim, in a happy, childlike voice: "That's it, Mama!" When the next stimulation, at #21, produced a convulsive tremor in the right leg, I placed the electrode on the instrument stand. "Okay," I said. "I think we've got enough. Suction, please."

The suction device was electrically powered, a thin transparent tube that operated like a vacuum cleaner. Over the years we had perfected its use so that we could control how much tissue it would draw. Naturally, in operations such as this, we wanted a minimal draw, one that would take no tissue beyond a depth of .05 millimeters and allow me to control the radius of excision by altering the suction tube's angle relative to the surface of the brain. I held it just off the perpendicular, about eighty degrees, then slowly cleared the area—some two millimeters in diameter—that lay within the circle of orange labels. Tissue and blood snaked quickly up the tube and flesh at the point of suction moved as if a wind had blown across its surface.

Crucial though it was, excision was the easiest part of this sort of operation. Five minutes after the last orange label had been placed, I returned the suction device to the instrument stand, disconnected my head-light, removed my gloves, offered my thanks to the staff and, leaving Eli to close the flap, headed for the door. I said good bye to Sarah, of course, but while her eyes flickered with obvious comprehension, she made no sound in reply. That did not surprise me. Even when language cells had not been removed, this sort of surgery often produced temporary muteness. Not only did swell-ing develop in the area adjacent to that excised, but also the routes and circuits of brain-cell connections were subjected to interruptions by the trauma of surgery in general. Something like short-circuits in an electrical system. I felt ninety percent sure that she'd be speaking again within forty-eight hours, and I estimated her chances of being seizure-free at somewhere between thirty and forty percent. Thinking back on it now, in fact, to the degree that thinking back is possible for me, or believable, I'd say that her prognosis then was not too much worse than my own.

Chapter Two

A lot of things changed in the next thirty minutes, and most of the changes reversed those that had preceded them. Whether things were improving or disimproving, coming together or falling apart, I couldn't say, but what they were for sure was unpredictable, discontinuous, what I used to call, in better days, "exciting." Of course, there are still days when I call this sort of thing "exciting," but for reasons that must be clear, I'm never altogether sure that my definition of "exciting" is correct or even, for that matter, consistent with definitions I have given it in the past. In fact, now that I think of it, with the exception perhaps of "brain damage," I can't think of any word that gives me more trouble than "exciting."

Did I feel "excited" when I left the operating room? Unless my memory betrays me, the answer is most emphatically no. I took a hard look at myself and what I saw was brain damage. How could I trust a brain that had not only forgotten my patient's name but claimed to have done so on purpose? On what grounds other than neurological dysfunction could "Oh Susannah!" be

explained? My symptoms seemed everywhere and unmistakable, and like any reasonable man, but more so,
of course, because of my clinical experience, I knew
that such symptoms, exciting or otherwise, could only
mean the worst for me.

But on my way to the locker room, I poured myself
a coffee from the machine we kept at the nurses' station,
and it lifted my spirits as much as mother had a few
minutes earlier. I had always been a coffee drinker—
ten to twelve cups on an average day—and, for that
very reason perhaps, always kept up with research on
caffeine. Yet I'd never appreciated as much as then the
potency of the compound, the way in which, trans-
forming one's neurochemistry, it could alter one's attitude toward oneself. Even before I'd finished the cup,
I had resumed my confidence and—as far as I was
concerned—my health. It was absolutely clear to me
that I wasn't suffering from brain damage. No dysfunction would leave one feeling as happy and optimistic
as I felt now. Furthermore, no neurological disease left
one with the capacity to evaluate his own behavior
with objectivity and detachment, and what was I doing
but that?

I had not forgotten my inappropriate behavior—"Oh
Susannah!" etc.—but thinking of it again, what I remembered most was the desire that had preceded it. It
seemed to me that a causal relationship existed between
this desire and the optimism I felt. Somehow, by choos-
ing to act as if I had brain damage, I had pointed myself
in the direction of happiness. By this act of supreme

will-power I had established a mastery over my brain. Again and again, I assured myself that all my actions had been and continued to be intentional. "Sarah" had been intentional, "Oh Susannah!" had been intentional, and now—as I became more and more bewildered by my thoughts—my confusion was intentional. In effect, whatever I did I wanted to do, and how many people whose brains are damaged can honestly tell you that?

In all my years as a neurosurgeon, I'd never heard of a *true* symptom that was *truly* intentional. I'd heard of fake symptoms that were intentional and real symptoms that patients believed intentional, but a real symptom, by definition, could not be intentional. The essence of a symptom is that the patient is powerless before it. One could not *choose* to be powerless because choice itself was power, choice itself was one's intention. Could you choose to do what you didn't choose to do? Maybe you'd think you didn't choose it, but by the time you did it, it was chosen. The moment you chose to do something, it was no longer what you didn't choose but what you did. The only way you could escape this circle was amnesia, a trick of the brain that allowed you, by forgetting your choices, to remember what you had chosen as what you hadn't, and thus to convince yourself, when the past became the future, that the wishes you'd fulfilled had in fact been disappointed.

An argument ensued between my father and my wife as to why, if my actions had been intentional, I had intended them. Why would a man of my position, a man not only conscientious about his work but devoted

to it, behave in such a manner as to undermine his
reputation? Was it perversity that drove me, a kind of
masochism? Was I driven for reasons as yet unknown
to sabotage myself? I couldn't follow much of what they
said, but it was my wife who got me pointed toward
the answer. It was her opinion that what appeared to
be symptoms was actually "rebellion," that I had begun
to realize, through a combination of instinct and insight,
that I was not my brain. In effect, I had had a sudden
vision of what she called my "real self," an essential
identity that was independent of my brain. This was
the reason for my confusion about what I had chosen
and what I hadn't. "Of course, a man can choose to do
what he doesn't choose to do," she explained. "All he
has to do is realize that the brain is the source of one
choice and he is the source of the other. Everything
he's doing becomes completely reasonable if you remember that he no longer believes, as the rest of us
do, that he and his brain are identical. Don't you see?
He's a liberated man! "Oh Susannah!" was his way of
saying no to his brain! 'No, I'm not behaving as you
expect me to behave! I'm not saying "Lucinda" just
because you tell me to! I'm not you! I'm not you! I'm
not you!' "

I was a little put off by her histrionics, but I had to
admit there was logic in her position. Knowing as much
as I did about the brain, how capricious the neurons
can be, how primitive and banal the vectors that lead
to memory and language, what could be more absurd
than defining oneself by its behavior? And what could

be more reasonable, once you had rejected this definition, than undercutting your brain, contradicting the
information it conveyed, saying "Lucinda" when it
wanted "Sarah," and then, once it got comfortable with
"Lucinda," going back to "Sarah" again? Because the
strength of the brain—I'd never seen this so clearly!—
resides in continuity, any sort of continuity. "Sarah" or
"Lucinda," it doesn't give a damn, as long as one or
the other endures. One thing you can be sure of, neurologically speaking, is that the enduring mistake will
always take precedence over a truth that's interrupted.
What the brain wants you to do is remember "Lucinda"
and say it again, and again, and if by chance you should
go back and forth—"Sarah," "Lucinda," "Sarah," "Lucinda," etc.—to accuse yourself, as I'd just done, of
illness, dysfunction, finally debasing yourself with the
ultimate epithet, "brain damage," which all our lives
the brain has used to frighten us into submission.

Wasn't it obvious? The brain defined "health" in a
manner that justified its authority, and then it defined
rejection of that authority as "disease"! And if by some
miracle a man came along who did not accept its definitions, a man for whom "brain damage," for example,
meant "adventure" or "freedom," it called such use of
language "confusion" or "incoherence" or even
"aphasia." And finally, as if that weren't enough, the
brain secreted emotions like fear and dread in support
of its positions, punishment meted out tenfold so as to
squelch all points of view that differed from its own.

Father, pointing out that all of these thoughts derived

from the very organ they presumed to discredit, bought
none of this. He knew my wife, and he'd always liked
her, but as he reminded me now, he had never deluded
himself as to her intelligence or maturity. An old neurosurgeon himself, he had fixed my career by taking
me into the operating room when I was twelve years
old. "What sort of misbegotten horseshit," he cried,
"could make you think that you are separate from your
brain? Your brain is your body, Izzy! Can you reject
your physical being? Your arms, your legs—can you
reject them? Just because your brain is capable of envisioning freedom from itself, does that make such freedom available? Don't you know that the brain can
envision anything? Even the absence of the vision it is
envisioning is not beyond its capabilities!"

I showered and dressed, then phoned my office to
dictate some notes on Sarah's operation to my secretary.
Heading for the elevator, I felt a sudden drop in my
energy, a kind of weakness in the knees that told me
(I always felt it first in my knees) that the caffeine was
wearing off. The speed of the brain's metabolism, its
ability to absorb compounds and consume the energy
they offered—it never ceased to amaze me. According
to recent research, the key ingredient in the caffeine-
response was a neurotransmitter called noradrenaline
which, through a combination of factors, caused an
increase in glucose production throughout the brain.
Glucose was an energy-source, but its metabolism was
almost as mercurial as that of noradrenaline itself. It
burned off quickly, and as it diminished, the effects

were felt throughout the central nervous system. Not just weakness in the knees but slower pulse and reflexes, lower blood pressure, and sometimes depression, hunger, anger, etc. One minute you're thinking one thing at a time, the next, two or three or four. In a matter of seconds, optimism becomes pessimism, self-confidence self-effacement, concentration distraction. All of this generated by what—250 milligrams of caffeine?

None of this was new to me, but as I pressed the button to summon the elevator, I told myself that the days were over when I would take it lying down. It infuriated me that my brain should be able to make me feel, as I felt now, so lethargic and depressed. Even if I were not yet able to reverse the pall it was casting over me, I sensed a new force within me, a confidence that someday, somehow, I'd find the will to resist its manipulations. The main thing was to be patient with myself, to remember that the road I'd taken was steep and full of obstacles. As mother pointed out, "Independence from the brain is not something that happens overnight. You don't just decide to do it—it takes work, Izzy! Courage and determination! Whatever happens, you mustn't forget—"

I lost track of her voice when the elevator came, but the spirit, the sense of her words stayed with me. Even without the help of caffeine, I felt encouraged. Though unclear about what I wanted to accomplish, I felt very determined, almost inspired, as if my goal were absolutely clear. In the elevator Kathy Wynne, a young nurse from the neurosurgical ward, stood arm in arm with Elizabeth Clinton, a tall, elderly patient who'd been admitted four days earlier. I knew they were coming from the radiology department because I'd ordered the brain-scan myself. Lizzy was a former college professor, an English teacher who in the last three weeks had lost forty years of her life. Sixty-five years old, tall, white-haired, with stooped shoulders and a heavily wrinkled face, she believed herself to be twenty-five, just completing work on her doctoral dissertation, and about to be married to her first husband, a professor of anthropology who'd been dead for eighteen years. We didn't know yet what her problem was, but we were hoping it was a brain tumor, which we might be able to treat, rather than one of the chronic, incurable diseases—Alzheimer's, for example, or Korsakoff's—which could also cause a retrograde amnesia. Since she had also lost her short-term memory and therefore responded to everyone, no matter how often she'd met them, as if she'd never seen them before, I was amazed at first when she spoke to me. Then I recalled that, like many patients with memory problems, she was embarassed and confused by her condition, and she tried to deny it by pretending recognition. In other words, she didn't remember but she remembered remembering, and she knew how to act as if she did. In fact, her greeting to me was identical to the one she offered every physician in the hospital.

"Hello, gorgeous."

"Hi, Lizzy."

She winked at me but spoke to Kathy. "Isn't he a hunk?"

When Kathy nodded, Lizzy shook her head up and down, then sideways, as if agreeing and disagreeing at the same time. She wasn't looking at me anymore. Her bright, distracted eyes were fixed on the floor-indicator above the elevator doors, watching the numbers change as if in disbelief. She had an extremely intelligent face, very inquisitive and probing, but it was always in motion, retreating from your glance like a face you saw in the window of a car that passed you on the street. Among her symptoms was one we called "Reduplication Syndrome," a not uncommon dysfunction that led her to see many things as copies of themselves. She was convinced that a perfect replica of this hospital existed directly across the street. Every day she ate six meals, and every nurse and doctor had a twin. What made her unusual (though not unique) among patients with this symptom was that her duplications, in certain cases, were slightly imperfect. For most such people reduplications were carbon copies, but for Lizzy the doctor or nurse who stood before her was always slightly more attractive than the twin she carried in her head. That's why she said to Kathy (though she was no longer looking at me and in all probability was just on the verge of forgetting I was there), "I'd take him over his brother any time, wouldn't you?"

There was music in the elevator, loudspeakers in the ceiling transmitting the same recorded tunes that played throughout the hospital. Christmas carols, though it was only the first week in December. The words SILENT NIGHT appeared, but it seemed to me they were not the ones I wanted. I had the words "Christmas carol," and I trusted them to be correct, but I had no doubt that "Silent Night" was not the title of the song. Furthermore, it seemed to me that "Silent Night" was not accidental. I had the distinct impression that certain cells had offered it perversely in order to interrupt the normal neurological circuits that might have offered the correct title. Was this to become a power struggle, an attempt by a single group of dysfunctional cells to seize control of my cortex? Especially painful was the sensation that even as I rejected "Silent Night" its replacement lurked just at the edge of my consciousness, floating in that realm we often call "the tip of my tongue."

Imagine facing a landscape you know to be beautiful, with a blindfold over your eyes, and you know how I felt about "Silent Night" and the title it blocked. Nor was I spared the need to correct my mistake which, of all neurological symptoms, may be the one that causes the greatest suffering. Healthy brains, when faced with lapses of this sort, greet them with equanimity. It's not too much to say that their greatest powers are negative— a tolerance for the absent, the unheard or the invisible, freedom from desire for inaccessible information. Brains like mine, on the other hand, are forever in search of things withheld, especially memories. Think of it as an attempt to eavesdrop through a corklined, insulated wall. Of memories as undeveloped photographs, emotions you want to feel but can't, food you smell but can't taste, shadows cast by objects you don't see. If the mark of a healthy brain is equanimity, one of the surest signs of brain disease is the rage and frustration, the hysteria, futility, the humiliation I felt at "Silent Night's" uninvited presence in my brain. It seemed that life could not continue until I replaced it with the title it impersonated, that the future must be delayed until the gap between myself and the "tip of my tongue" was closed. Tell me please: what neurological force determined that I must honor the need I felt to retrieve the title but ignore the other voices, so much more reasonable, which advised me (1) that the name of this song was of no importance to me, and (2) that as long as I persisted in the quest for it, that quest was guaranteed to fail? Easy to say that one part of my brain was determined to remember the title while another was determined to forget it, but more important was the violent resistance that each of these parts aroused in the other. For the more I tried to forget the title the more I needed to remember it, and the more I needed to remember it, the more inaccessible it became.

Curious too that I never questioned my belief that "Silent Night" was incorrect. Why did I think that a brain that could not perform a simple act of identification should nevertheless be capable of this function, so much more complex, which allowed it to discriminate between true and false? If my brain were really damaged, wasn't it possible that the real symptom was that which had denied "Silent Night" its credibility? How many patients had I seen who suffered from this—an

inability to trust their memories? Whatever they remembered they believed invented, and even when their
memory functioned perfectly, they lived with the fear
that something had been forgotten. You'd see them
standing in the ward, scratching their heads, asking
themselves, sometimes out loud, "What was it?" and if
you asked them what they meant by "it," they wouldn't
be able to answer. In retrospect, it seems to me quite
possible that, like them, I suffered less from amnesia
than fear of it, less from a primary disorder than a
secondary one, which had crippled the part of my brain
that produced evaluations of itself. If that were the case,
it was no surprise that "Silent Night" had disappointed
me. Since people with this condition are as often satisfied when they ought to be disappointed as disappointed when they ought to be satisfied, whatever I did
would disappoint me except that with which I had no
reason to be satisfied.

I had entered the elevator at the third floor, and the
song I called "Silent Night" ended at the fifth. The doors
opened here, at the Psychiatric Ward, but the man who
stood outside, a middle-aged patient in a blue-and-white
dressing gown, either changed his mind or couldn't
make it up or maybe just amused himself like this,
calling for the elevators. By the time the doors had
closed again, "Winter Wonderland" was playing. That
in its case I was unambivalent, offered no solace. In
fact, as the elevator rose again, I felt a kind of panic
that "Winter Wonderland" might obscure the song it
had displaced before I could identify it. And of course,

no sooner did I fear forgetting than I forgot. Is there
any game the brain enjoys like the self-fulfilling proph-
ecy? Within an instant I knew that, just as I'd feared,
I was losing the melody I'd hoped to maintain. I tried
humming it to myself, but it slipped in and out of my
grasp until it lost all connection with the tune it had
once been, the tune it was meant to be. Thus I found
myself in the ridiculous position of longing for a song
of which I could remember neither the title nor the
tune.

"What was that song?" I cried.

"What song?" Kathy said.

"The one that was just playing!"

Lizzy smiled at me demurely, nodding as if with
sympathy and understanding. "My favorite song," she
said, "is 'Home on the Range'."

"Goddammit, I don't care about 'Home on the Range'!
I want the song that was playing before!"

"Where?" Kathy said.

"What do you mean 'where'?" I pointed to the speaker
above me. "There!"

Kathy shrugged. "Oh, Lord, I'm afraid you're asking
the wrong person. I never listen to Muzak. It's in one
ear and out the other!"

It had already been noted on Lizzy's chart that songs
of her childhood, those that pre-dated the period erased
by her amnesia, were her favorite means of entertaining
herself. Sitting around the ward, she was always humming or singing, her voice brittle and childlike but
always on-key and strangely, almost unbearably, mel-

lifluous, her memory for lyrics (which according to most
neurological theory are stored in different regions of the
brain than those responsible for conceptual information)
impeccable. Once a song came into her head, nothing
could stop her from singing it, so it was no surprise to
Kathy or me when she gave us "Home on the Range."

> Home, home on the Range!
> Where the deer and the antelope play!
> Where seldom is heard,
> A discouraging word,
> And the skies are not cloudy all day!

While she was singing, I found her voice extremely
irritating, but when she was done I noticed with amazement that its effect upon my brain had been medicinal.
To put it simply, my disabilities fell away. By the time
the elevator reached our floor, I had made a complete
turnabout. God knows what was going on. Was it possible that a song as banal as this could affect one's
neurochemistry, or had she lured my brain in the direction of health by diverting it from itself? Whatever
the reason, there was nothing on the tip of my tongue.
More than irrelevant, the issue of "Silent Night" was
suddenly laughable. I looked back on my amnesia as
one might on a fit of sneezing or a slip on a banana
peel, and as for the antagonism I'd felt with regard to
my brain, it was replaced by a sense of kinship and
cooperation, trust, as if its voice and my own were once
again identical. And as so often happens in dealings

with one's brain, the more I believed it friendly, the more like a friend it pretended to be. Conviction mounted on behalf of "Silent Night." Suddenly I knew that it had always been correct! As for its lack of credibility, the perverse, irrational doubt with which it had been surrounded, I saw it as a trap into which I'd been lured by ideas of the sort that my wife had propagated. Father's wisdom, how on earth could I doubt it? The idea that one could reject his brain—what could it lead to but doubt and fear, paranoia of the sort I'd just escaped? Could anyone in his right mind idealize such disorder?

With the evening meal already served and visiting hours not yet begun, the ward was very quiet, no sounds except patients' television sets and the ubiquitous Muzak, now from the speakers in the hall. At the freight elevator, an orderly leaned against a metal cart stacked with used dinner trays, and a post-op patient I didn't know shuffled down the hall, wheeling the portable intravenous stand plugged into his wrist. It seemed to me that the scratching sound made by his slippers on the white linoleum floor generated feelings of euphoria, but that was because I had forgotten, for the moment, that I was almost always euphoric on the ward. It is not too much to say that these surroundings had an effect on my brain almost identical to that of caffeine. With my authority and competence taken for granted, a whole staff awaiting my commands, every bed occupied by someone who needed me, how could my brain perform with anything less than optimum health?

There, as in the operating room, I remembered only
what I needed to remember. My thoughts moved at a
steady pace, "one thing," as we say, "leading to another." I hadn't the slightest interest in their origins. I
won't say that I never paused to search for words, or
that the information I needed was always at hand, but
when the word or the fact wasn't there, I took its absence
in stride. In effect, as far as I was concerned, my brain
did not exist, and if there's a better definition of neurological health, I don't know what it is.

I went to my office and checked the mail, made a
few phone calls, then headed for the nurses' station.
The chief nurse was organizing the evening medication
cart, and Eli was lounging with his feet on the desk. It
struck me that his name was Elmore, but not with
sufficient force to make me say it aloud. In fact, I
decided, because of the doubt, to avoid his name altogether. Eating a candy bar and sipping a cup of coffee,
he was still wearing the clothes he'd worn in the operating room. Here and there the trousers were marked
with trickles of blood that looked like needle-point.

"How's Lucinda?" I said.

" 'Sarah,' " he said. "Stop fucking around, boss."

"How is she?"

"Sound asleep. Like a baby. You think we got it all?"

"Sure," I said.

I didn't know what he meant by "it" and I certainly
didn't know what I meant by "sure," but more and
more I knew that "Elmore" was correct. I studied him

closely, as if I'd never seen him before. He was thirty–five
years old, tall, wiry, with sunken cheeks, shoulder-
length hair, and the pale, yellowish skin one develops
from spending too much time in the hospital. He had
a hand-tremor, probably hereditary, a type that derives
from the Thalamic Region of the brain. One day we'd
go in and fix it for him. The technology wasn't there
yet, but it was on the way. In the meantime, he was
causing problems in the department. With patients he
tried to keep his hands in his pockets, but sometimes
he had to take them out, and then, of course, he didn't
inspire a lot of confidence in his operating technique.
What they didn't know was the most amazing thing
about his tremor—that it disappeared when he was
operating. On a bad day he could barely button his
shirt, but in the OR he was as meticulous and de-
pendable as anyone in the department. Not too long
ago, we'd written this up and published it in the *Journal*.
Why should a neurological problem appear and disappear according to circumstance? No one could answer
that question, but the facts were indisputable. When
his hand held a scalpel, it didn't shake at all.

Spread out on the desk were the Polaroid shots produced by Lizzy's brain scan. These were black-and-
white photographs taken directly off the computer screen,
information relayed from a camera that took its pictures
while rotating around a patient's head. A fairly recent
innovation, it was the best technique we had for ana-
lyzing brain tissue and therefore the surest read we
could get on whether Lizzy had a tumor.

"How's it look?" I said, nodding toward the pictures.
"No sign of a tumor," he said.
"Damn, I was afraid of that. Well, maybe she had a
bleed. Take her down for an angiogram on Monday."
"A bleed?" Eli laughed. "C'mon, Izzy. You know she
didn't have a bleed. It's Alzheimer's or Korsakoff's. You
know that as well as I do."
"Maybe I do, Elmore, and maybe I don't. In any event,
if it wouldn't inconvenience you too much, I'd like to
see her angiogram."
" 'Elmore'?"
"What?"
"What'd you call me?"
"Why do you ask?"
He glanced at me quizzically, closing his right eye
and munching on his candy. It's never easy to think
what he was thinking, but it's especially hard when
the person you're thinking it about happens to be your
boss. Watching him weigh the matter, I felt for a moment
that I could see all this—a sort of neurological alarm
system—developing in his brain. I saw one group of
cells sounding the alarm, another deciding whether to
heed it, yet another reviewing my behavior to see why
the alarm had sounded in the first place. A sort of
electoral process, a combination of chemistry and elec-
tricity that worked like a parimutual machine. Father
suggested I might be hallucinating, but I felt proud of
what I saw, very excited, as if my vision had sharpened
or I were travelling in a world that had always been
off-limits to me.
A pile of charts lay on the desk, and I picked up the

one on top. It belonged to a man named Herman Ed-
dingoff, who was suffering from a malignant tumor, one
of those that within a couple of months could occupy
three-quarters of the skull. In general, it took just about
that much time to kill. "How's Herman?" I said.

Though Elmore's discomfort was clearly visible now,
he leapt at the chance to change the subject. He pointed
his thumb at the floor. "His wife has signed a release
for his eyes and kidneys."

"Ha, ha, ha."

Authentic though it sounded, this was not, in my
opinion, laughter, but rather an involuntary explosion,
an outburst of tics or muscle twitches. Odd sensations
circulated. My head seemed very heavy, as if my neck
and shoulders were taxed by the weight that they supported. I moved my shoulders forward and back, then
rolled my head in a wide, deliberate circle and stretched
it forward and down until my chin was resting on my
chest. To my amazement, I actually expected that this
would make me feel better. As if my brain would be
calmed by rotations on its axis.

Elmore stared at me. He'd taken a bite of his candy,
but he kept it in his cheek without chewing. Clearing
my throat loudly, I reached in the pocket of my ward
coat and removed my reflex hammer and tapped it
three or four times in my left palm. This was a gesture
that had always focussed my thoughts, but it did nothing
for me now.

"What about the autopsy?" I said.

"She's agreed to that as well."

I was slightly bewildered by this exchange, not only his answer but my question, but I still believed that any minute, if I continued to say whatever came into my mind, I would know what I was doing. As it turned out, I was incorrect. The more I spoke, the more I felt as if my mind were leaving my brain behind, or vice-versa. When I spoke I heard my voice as if on a tape-delay, and what I said, while it made sense to me, came as a complete surprise.

"Tell Pathology to expect his brain. That's an unusual tumor he's got. It'd be nice to study the cells at next week's conference."

Elmore took out his notebook and wrote himself a reminder. His hands were shaking, but the pencil calmed them like a scalpel. My thoughts were racing. Imagine standing in the middle of a turnpike with traffic speeding by on both sides, zip, zip, zip, and you know how I felt about my thoughts. Still gripping the hammer, I sat down at the desk beside him. I put it in my right pocket, then took it out and put it in my left, then took it out again and returned it to my right. Desperate now, I took it out of my pocket and placed it on the desk and lay my right hand flat on top of it. Nothing worked. If anything, thought increased—not only its speed and quantity but also the hope I felt as each thought arrived. It was almost as if I expected each in turn to be my last. Finally, I placed my right forefinger in my nostril and pressed it high up against the bridge of my nose. I knew at once that this was what I'd been searching for. Happiness swept me like a wave. I felt optimistic, determined, and finally, contemplative, as if now my mind would give me what I asked of it. Great numbers of cells in my brain had been milling about like a crowd, but now they lined up, organized and obedient, like soldiers on parade.

"Do you want a tissue?" Eli said.

"What do you mean, 'tissue'?"

He pulled one from a box on the desk and offered it to me.

"No thanks," I said.

On Saturday nights, with the weekend schedule in effect, we didn't make rounds, but went through the patients by way of their charts. The ward population was more or less typical of the patients we saw most of the time: four malignant tumors and five benign; six aneurysms; eight epileptics being evaluated for seizure surgery. We had three people scheduled for lobotomy— two for psychological reasons and one for intractable pain—and two with tumors on their spinal cords. In room 1640 we had Peter McCarthy, an ex-welder whose head had been smashed by a steel girder. Though severely amnesic and subject to fits of violence, he seemed indifferent to his problem, referring to the crevice in his forehead as his "ashtray," laughing aloud when his memory failed him, or stating to those he encountered on the ward: "Without memory, brother, forget it." According to his wife and children, he'd had no sense of humor before his accident, but he kept the whole ward laughing now. Sharing his room was Arnold Klosterman, a seventy-year-old psychoanalyst with a malig-

nant tumor who spoke a garbled language we called
"word salad." "Tell you what I want you to want, right?
Insight, insight, it's all very clear. Pay for your sessions,
why not? Take charge of your life! The brain? The
brain? How many times have I heard that excuse?" We
had one person with Tourette's Syndrome, a diffuse
condition that produced outbursts of profanity; three
who were completely mute; and one who described
everything he did as he did it: "I'm getting out of bed
now . . . my feet are touching the floor . . . what have
I done with my slippers? Oh yes, here they are. I'll put
my feet inside them and now I'll stand up."

As usual too, there were anomalies that had aroused
the interest of neurologists and neurophysiologists from
other hospitals as well as our own. One of the stroke
patients had a paralyzed left arm that rose to her mouth
whenever she yawned. One of the non-malignant tumors was located in a region between brain hemispheres, causing a lack of communication between the
two halves of the patient's brain, a condition called the
"Split-Brain Syndrome," which led the patient to frequent bouts of contradictory behavior. He could pull
on his pants with one hand and push them down with
the other, spit out food he thought he liked, or freeze
when walking down the hall because half his brain
wanted exercise while the other half was ready for bed.

As I say, nothing unusual about this group of patients—I'd been treating people like this for twenty-five
years. But during the course of this review, I realized
that there had been a dramatic shift in the perspective

from which I viewed them. For me, they were no longer victims of the brain but rebels against it, revolutionaries, people who'd taken a stand against the tyranny to which normal people—Eli and me, for example—acquiesced like slaves. What could be sillier than he and I sitting in judgment upon people like Peter and Dr. Klosterman, calling them "sick" when in fact they'd taken the path of truth and courage? Naturally, Father was disgusted by these thoughts, but I held firm against him. As you see, I'd once again accepted the anti-brain position advocated by my wife. I saw the brain as a tyrant and those with brain damage as people who had escaped it.

I was skeptical about this position, of course, but I realized that skepticism itself was a product of my brain. How else, except skeptical, would one expect the brain to feel about thoughts that undermined its authority? I guess it could be said that ideas accumulating all afternoon had now matured into their unavoidable conclusion and this conclusion, like the thoughts that had produced it, lacked any sign of reason or coherence. Obviously I was not unaware of this, but such was my conviction that signs of its illogic gave it greater strength. Logic being the brain's own invention, how could I not take faith from indications of its absence?

Leaving Eli, I ran into Lizzy again. She was out for an evening stroll in the hall, hesitating between steps, staring straight ahead with the same bewildered expression I'd seen in the elevator, touching the wall as she walked, like so many of her fellow-patients did, as if by that means to locate herself in space. Euphoric now with the effects of my thoughts, I concluded suddenly, for no reason whatsoever, that I owed them to her. She was my teacher, my guide, the one who had helped me break away from my brain. There ensued a rush of affection that made me very angry at her. Why angry? Because I was worried about myself, frightened of my condition, and most important, listening to father again.

"For God's sake!" he cried. "Pull yourself together! Brain damage is not a game!"

"Hello, handsome," Lizzy said.

"Go fuck yourself," I said.

"Where's your brother?"

"I don't have a brother."

She giggled flirtatiously. "Come on, silly. Don't play games with me."

"Game? Brain damage is not a game, Lizzy."

"Of course it isn't. Don't you think I know that?"

My anger was extreme, but the word I found for it was "gratitude." Since I recognized that "gratitude" was incorrect but held to it anyway, I could not avoid suspecting myself (for the first time) of aphasia, but my suspicions neither disturbed me nor sent me in search of language ("anger," to be specific) to allay them. In fact, "gratitude," it seemed to me, was an act of faith as well as courage. Defiance collected behind it, so much so that I began to think it might be correct. The warmth I felt for Lizzy reminded me of feelings I'd had for my sister.

"Since when do you have a sister?" Mother said.

I grabbed Lizzy by the shoulders. "Look at me, dammit! Who am I?"

"How should I know? I never saw you in my life."

"If you never saw me, how do you know I have a brother?"

"What?" Lizzy's nose wrinkled adorably. I don't know if it was a perceptual distortion on my part or a youthfulness derived from brain damage, but at that moment she looked like a five-year-old.

"You heard me. You say I have a brother and then you say you don't know me. How do you know I have a brother when you don't know who I am? Come on, Lizzy! Make up your mind!"

She took a step back and raised her hands as if I'd threatened her. "Listen, young fella, you'd better watch yourself. I've had just about enough of you! One more step and I'll report you to the authorities."

"Authorities? What authorities?" For some reason I felt very friendly toward her again. "What a load of shit," I said.

"That's more like it," Lizzy said. "Does it hurt to be a gentleman?"

I closed my eyes, took a deep breath and held it. When I opened my eyes, I was surprised to find her in front of me. That is to say, I had no memory—none whatsoever—of any previous conversation between us.

"Hey Lizzy!" I cried. "How are you?"

"Very well, thank you. And you?"

"What brings you to the hospital?"

"What hospital? This is not a hospital. I am visiting friends in the country."

"And your health? How's your health?"

"I have a few complaints, naturally, but at my age, you've got to expect such things."

"How old are you?"

"Twenty-five, I'll be twenty-six in May."

Grabbing her shoulders again, I shook her violently. "You're lying, goddammit. You're sixty-five years old, Lizzy."

"What's that? Sixty-five? What is this—some sort of joke?"

"No, it's not a joke. It's *reality!*" I tapped her on the forehead. "Your problem is right here! You've lost your memory! Three pounds of flesh in this skull, that's where your problem is! You *think* you're twenty-five, but you're *really* sixty-five! You *think* you're visiting friends, but you're *really* in the hospital! Your problem is here, Lizzy! Your brain is telling you lies!"

Lizzy backed away. For a moment she looked as if I'd struck her, but then her face emptied and flattened, becoming inanimate, like a photo of itself. Her laugh sounded hollow at first, but as she turned away from me and headed for her room, it became a belly laugh that echoed through the halls. She yelled at me over her shoulder. "That's a good one! Now, that is pretty good. I don't know who you are, young fella, but you sure have a sense of humor!"

I watched her with a smile, then all at once ran after her. "Hey, Lizzy!" I cried. "Wait up!"

I didn't know what I wanted to say to her, but I began to speak even before I'd caught her. "Listen, Lizzy, I'm sorry. I really didn't mean—"

She stopped in her tracks without turning. Coming round in front of her, I saw that the face that had been so vacant just seconds before was radiant, almost beatific. Not five years old, not sixty-five; she looked about the age she thought she was: twenty-five.

"Hello, handsome," she said.

CHAPTER THREE

Next morning, while my wife was making coffee, I decided not to move. I saw it as a clear-cut decision, a choice I could neither explain nor resist. Father, as might be expected, saw it differently. What I called a decision he called an incapacity. "I don't want to go into the decision-making process," he said, "the neurology of Frontal Lobe behavior and all that, but time and again the research has demonstrated that motor behavior takes precedence over will-power. A man can no more will himself in the direction of paralysis than he can will himself not to breathe. The needs of the body simply cannot be malnourished." It seemed to me that he was aware of his mistake, but still, I was grateful to mother for pointing it out. " 'Malnourished'?" she laughed. "Just because he's incoherent doesn't mean that you should not be recalcitrant. Who said decided not to anything? About breathing? All he said is move, and who are you to play this kind of nourishment reasoning instead of?"

I was not yet so far gone as to miss the point they were missing. The real question, it seemed to me, was

whether the decision I claimed to have made had preceded or succeeded my paralysis. In other words,
whether I could not or did not wish to move, whether
I was paralyzed or stubborn or perhaps merely lazy,
whether *my brain* or *I myself* had restricted my mobility,
whether my problem was finally to be classified as
"neurological" or "psychological." Needless to say, it
was not a question with which I was unfamiliar. Very
often, with brain-damaged patients, the first and perhaps
the greatest issue is such delegation of responsibility.
Who's boss, in other words, you or your brain? Some
patients think they're doing everything, some nothing,
and some go back and forth, telling themselves one
minute that their brain is the cause of their mistakes,
the next that—through ignorance, perversity, laziness
or some other shortcoming—they've no one to blame
but themselves. Among the latter group there are those
who draw so much inspiration from the psychological
position that they often claim responsibility where none
is justified. Inflicted with amnesia, they blame themselves as if by an act of will or concentration their
memory will improve. "Think, dammit, what was her
name?" If they try to talk and word salad comes out,
they curse themselves as one might for overeating, cowardice or laziness. In effect, their symptoms make them
feel guilty. People of the opposite inclination, on the
other hand, feel no guilt at all. Why should they when,
as they see it, their brains are doing everything? When
even laziness or selfishness is neurochemical? Blaming
yourself for what your brain is doing is like blaming

yourself for the behavior of a stranger. This sort of patient, nothing makes him so happy as proof that his brain is damaged.

My wife was a small woman with very broad shoulders and hair cut short like a boy's. She wore unmatched earrings, a single pearl in the left ear and a gold loop in the right. On her left forearm was a small tattoo of the Yin-Yang symbol that she'd got in Kathmandu, fourteen years before, when she was working in Tibetan refugee camps. I didn't know her name but I was convinced it began with "M." In an attempt to jog my memory, I made a list—"Martha, Marjorie, Mary, Millie, Marlene, Melissa, Margaret," and (not realizing my mistake) "Nancy"—but not one of these names elicited that happy sensation the brain secrets when the proper box has been opened and such perverse hide-and-seek games are foiled. Feeling bereft, just on the verge of panic, in fact, I made a conscious, a willful decision, embracing "Martha" with conviction that was transparent in its insincerity, thinking "Martha, Martha, Martha, Martha, Martha," as if to seduce my brain, as if by repetition it could be persuaded of what it knew to be incorrect.

She placed my mug on my night-table, then climbed into bed beside me. As the aroma of coffee spread through the room, I felt a tremendous desire for it, but this desire had an inverse effect, strengthening my original decision not to move. I knew I'd feel better if I drank my coffee, so much so perhaps that decisions of the sort that had arrested my movement would pass through my brain without arousing the slightest interest, much less attachment, much less a need to act on them; but the very image of such improvement made the thought of coffee abhorrent. Soon its aroma lost its appeal, becoming bitter, acidic, almost nauseating.

Thus did I discover that my olfactory cells were also participating in my collapse. I no longer had any interest in distinguishing between different causes for my immobility, whether I could not or would not move, whether movement was possible and rejected or impossible and believed to be rejected. The indisputable fact was that I wasn't moving. Several times the wish to move seemed actually to crystallize within me—I saw myself sitting up, for example, drinking my coffee, talking to Martha, etc.—but such visions led to nothing. I had an idea my body was stiffening, edging toward rigidity, but even the fact that the sensation was unpleasant did not prevent my being happy about it. Had I already attained the freedom that so many brain-damaged patients achieve, the state of mind in which discomfort itself becomes a source of happiness?

A new voice appeared. Though often repetitive and strident, it had confidence and authority, even omniscience. In fact, it was my own thoughts it seemed to be voicing. Even when I disagreed with it, it seized my interest and attention. It was almost as if, alone among my voices, it did not originate in my brain. How is it, I asked myself, that certain regions of the brain seem to be outside it? I was thinking of the cells that produce the pronouns "I" or "me," the whole idea of what one calls "myself." When you tell yourself, for example,

"Pull yourself together!" which cells are talking and which are they addressing? Now I really felt excited. Of all the questions brain damage had offered me, none seemed deeper or more important than these, none so worthy of investigation. I swore to myself that if I ever got better I'd devote myself to researching them, but even as I made this vow, I suspected that, if I really got better, such questions would never occur to me.

It was the premise of this voice that my decision not to move was less about paralysis than brain damage in general. It wasn't just immobility I wanted to explore but the whole world of neurological incapacity. Unlike mother and father, this voice considered the decision not only rational but courageous, a natural outgrowth of my lifelong scientific and clinical preoccupations. Having studied the brains of others, I had now determined to study my own, and what better way to do that than by cultivating symptoms? "What can we learn from a normal brain?" it cried. "If words appear whenever we need them, what do we learn about the cells that have produced them? It's only the failing brain that reveals its secrets to us. Every symptom is a mine of information! This is why I delight in my amnesia! This is why I'm not moving now! What you see before you is not neurological dysfunction but neurological research!"

But consider the speed of the brain! This dialogue, as I understood it, required less than one or two seconds. The words seemed to occur all at once instead of one after another, as if, like a photographic image, they'd originated, not in the language regions of my brain, but in the Optic Lobe. By the time Marjorie spoke to me, it was all complete and stored in my memory, a source of fear already that it might be forgotten.

"Drogin? Are you awake? Please sit up. I've got to talk to you."

Legs drawn up so as to form the blanket into a tent with her knees, she cradled her coffee at her chest and stared at it with a concentration that seemed to me willful, almost maniacal. She always used the same mug, a blue-and-white striped ceramic with a handle large enough for all her fingers. Looming over me, she looked much taller than I remembered, also stronger and, now I think of it, a bit intimidating. A single tear moved slowly over her cheek and fell onto the shoulder of my t-shirt, the old yellow t-shirt she used as a nightgown. Given my condition, it's no surprise that I saw this tear as a neurological event, not an indication of emotion, even persisted in this point of view after mother berated me for it and father, in a halfhearted attempt to defend me, explained that "coldness" and "detachment" were typical of those with brain damage. "Once your brain has betrayed you," he said, "it's very hard to trust it. And if you can't trust it, how can you feel what ordinary people feel? How can you be a *true human being?*"

"We've got to talk," Martha said, and then, "Dammit, sit up, will you? This is serious."

She looked down at me, smiling in spite of herself. Tears came heavily now. As often when she was upset, her voice was thin and slightly whiny, a bit like a ten-year-old's. "It's no good anymore between us. We've got to let go. I know you've heard me say this before, but this time I mean it. I've got to get a place of my own. I can't postpone it any longer. I feel like I'm dying! Wasting my life! I've got to learn to be alone, take care of myself. If I don't connect with myself, how can I connect with you? I'm not saying I don't love you. But it's all habit now, mechanical, automatic, look how we fucked last night, no passion, just going through the motions, I don't blame you, I blame myself."

She'd stopped crying now. As she sipped her coffee, her eyes were shining with excitement, and her face was fierce, defiant and slightly playful, one eye squinting now and then as if aiming at a target. With every word she spoke her voice grew stronger and clearer until the whine disappeared and she sounded her age again. It wasn't divorce she wanted, she said, just a year or two of "partial separation." Maybe we'd see each other for dinner or an occasional weekend. Even sex if we felt like it. We didn't have to be rigid about it. Who knows? Maybe with space between us, solitude and privacy, we'd appreciate each other again, stop taking each other for granted. Why should we let our marriage disintegrate the way most marriages did? If we really loved each other, we had to find a way to be lovers again.

While she was talking, another symptom had appeared. I was thinking more than one thing at a time. At least two and sometimes three or four. No sooner did I start in one direction than I headed in another—

a constant stream of interruption, thoughts interrupted by secondary thoughts, secondary thoughts interrupted, etc. Most of the time I could not remember what I'd been thinking even seconds before. I kept asking myself, "What was I thinking?" but far from settling my thoughts, or rather settling me on a single thought, such questions became another interruption. In the midst of such babble, Martha's voice became, for all intents and purposes, inaudible. How could I follow her thoughts when I couldn't follow my own? Though she went on for several minutes, I heard nothing more until she realized I wasn't listening.

"Jesus Christ, where the fuck are you? Would you please tell me where you are? Jesus Christ!" She threw off the covers, got out of bed and stalked out of the room. On the way to the "roof," I figured, meaning "bathroom." I heard her cursing me—"Motherfucker, sonofabitch, cocksucker," etc.—but by the time she returned, she'd turned her anger on herself. "Okay, I get it. If I were you, I wouldn't listen either. I've been saying this for years, right? I'm full of shit, right? Self-centered, spoiled, neurotic, why should you listen? Well, goddammit, I'm tired of being this way! I don't want it anymore! This time, you'll see . . . I mean it! How can I change, living with you? Our marriage is . . . a womb! Yes, that's it—a womb! Comfort and safety and whatever I do you approve of. How can I change when I feel so secure? I'm hiding behind you, Izzy. You're my father and my mother. If I don't have the guts to let go of you, I'll stay a child forever."

I noticed now that in the bathroom she'd put on her white karate training suit—her "gi." On weekday mornings, she went to her karate school, what they called the "dojo," before she went to work, but on Sundays she went in the afternoon and did her morning workout at home. She'd removed her earrings and put on a red headband. Her black belt hung on her shoulder, but now, facing the mirror on the back of the bedroom door, she tied it on with an air of solemnity, knotting it, looping it, centering it precisely below her navel.

"You're not getting up?" she said.

"No," I said.

"Are you all right?"

"I don't know. I think I have brain damage."

"So? Who doesn't?"

Crossing the room, she bowed before the altar she'd set up on a small table in the corner. It consisted of a small jade Buddha, a ceramic water bowl, a vase containing a single golden lilly, and a bronze, sand-filled Tibetan incense stand. Lighting a stick of incense, she centered it carefully in the stand, then pressed her palms together and bowed again. Finally, kneeling, she sat back on her calves, and with palms cupped in her lap, thumbs touching, commenced her workout as she always did, with two minutes of meditation.

On the pillow, my head moved slowly from side to side, and a smile spread over my face. This was automatic behavior, as I understood it, nothing to do with me. Still, it was not without its repercussions. Eli's voice joined mother's and father's and the one I called my

own, and the latter insisted that, once and for all, I
diagnose myself. "Begin at the beginning!" it cried. "Is
this brain damage or hysteria? Research or pathology?
Are you faking it? Enjoying it? Is it panic you feel or
an interest in panic?" Unable to answer any of these
questions, I decided to take its advice and examine
myself as if I were one of my patients. If I were truly
brain damaged, I would admit it, and if I weren't, I
would stop pretending that I was.

"What's your name?"

"Isaac Drogin."

"Address?"

"I don't know."

"How old are you?"

"Forty-four."

"Height?"

"Five-nine."

"Weight?"

"One fifty-five."

"What color eyes?"

"Brown."

"Hair?"

"Blond."

"Where were you born?"

"I don't know."

"Yes, you do."

"No, I don't."

"What's your work?"

"Neurosurgeon."

"Where?"

"The hospital."
"Which hospital?"
"I don't know."
"You're lying."
"I know."
"Why?"
"I don't know."

Millie had begun her stretching exercises, a routine she'd learned in India, when for a time she'd been a student of Hatha Yoga. Beginning with her palms pressed together at her chest, she closed her eyes, then spread her arms, arched her back, kneeled with hands beside her knees, stretched her legs behind her, dropped her chest to the floor, raised her hips, straightened her legs, spread her arms and arched her back again, then finally finished as she'd begun, with palms together at her chest. Each movement was accompanied by an audible inhalation or exhalation. She repeated this four times, then moved on to other postures: a headstand, a shoulderstand, a spinal twist to each side, and finally, a series of breathing exercises.

Sitting back on her heels, she pressed her thumb against her right nostril, inhaled for approximately ten seconds through her left, and then held her breath for nearly a minute. Then she lifted her thumb and closed her left nostril with her ring finger and exhaled for maybe twenty seconds through her right. Keeping her fingers in the same position, she inhaled through her right nostril and exhaled through her left. Six times she repeated the series until finally, completing the

warmup as she always did, she closed her eyes and lay
on her back with her hands palm up at her sides. She
remained like this for four or five minutes, and then,
still motionless on the carpet, out of my line of sight,
she called to me:

"Are you awake?"

"Yes," I said.

"What's happoning?"

"Nothing."

"How's the brain damage?"

"Fine," I said.

Standing now, she began her karate practice, a workout her teacher had designed for use at home. Watching
herself carefully in the mirror on the back of the bedroom door, she did front-kicks and back-kicks and side-
kicks and one kick that began at the floor and snapped
like a whip at a point above her head. Each kick was
repeated at least ten and sometimes as many as twenty
times, and each was accompanied by a forced, audible
exhalation that sounded like the respirator we used in
surgery. She practiced different kinds of punches with
each hand, blocking maneuvers with her legs and arms,
and then she did a whole series of exercises to loosen
her pelvic and shoulder sockets. Perspiring freely but
not breathing hard, she practiced the knife-hand punch
that was used, she had once explained to me, to put
out an opponent's eye or to strike the center of his
neck; worked on block-punch combinations and concluded her preliminary workout with yet another
breathing exercise—a wide-mouthed inhalation fol-

lowed by a forced exhalation in which she squeezed her stomach and abdomen to expel as much air as possible. She repeated this perhaps a dozen times, holding her breath longer with each repetition, exhaling with greater force, and her face grew progressively redder and more contorted with effort until, in the last few repetitions, it looked to be in pain.

I was not displeased with my examination, but a certain uneasiness had followed several of my answers. Not, surprisingly, "I don't know," but rather "blond" and "brown" as well as, to a lesser extent, "five-nine." Each of these had produced, almost instantly, feelings of discomfort and disappointment and a larger, more diffuse sensation, something akin to, but a bit more severe, than shame. Did this mean that my hair was not "blond," my eyes not "brown," my height not "five-nine"? Had I been less professional, or a bit more impatient, I would have accepted this conclusion—that I suffered from an amnesic condition that caused me to lose such information as my height and the color of my eyes—without looking further. For there was no arguing the fact that a man who called himself "blond" when blond was not the color of his hair, would experience (provided that the true color of his hair continued to reside in his accessible memory) a sensation not unlike the one I felt. What I knew, however, was that, under certain neurological conditions, even a man whose hair is blond can experience uneasiness upon describing himself as such. For one thing, in certain forms of brain damage the neurology of disappointment is itself askew.

Even the most impeccable behavior leaves you feeling like a failure because one part of the brain has expected something that another has failed to produce. What makes this problem especially difficult is that one doesn't know whether the disappointment has arisen out of dysfunction in the region that expects or the region that produces. Where a word like "blond" is concerned, you can't tell, until you've actually pinpointed the source of your brain damage, whether your disappointment is valid or invalid, proof that "blond" is incorrect or a sign that, even though it isn't, the chemistry of disappointment has been initiated in your brain.

This is not to say that I had discounted the possibility that my disappointment was justified, having arisen out of the fact that "blond" was simply not the color of my hair. But in this case, a whole different range of dysfunctions had to be considered. "Blond" could be caused by amnesia or aphasia or a combination of the two, a memory defect that caused me to remember my hair as blond even though it wasn't, or a language problem that led me, even though I remembered my hair as brown, for example, or red, or purple, to call it "blond" because I believed that "blond" *meant* "brown" or "red" or "purple."

For all the precision of this analysis, however, I knew that I had yet to consider the really difficult, the fearful possibilities, the diagnoses that left the realm of language or memory and entered those of choice and will power, that vast neurological limbo in which illusions of personal control are generated and refined. In the case of "five-nine," for example, was it not possible that I knew myself to be, say "five-six" but described myself as taller because I *wished* to be? A good neurologist never forgets that, if true-false discrimination is an innate function of the brain, the *desire for truth* is equally so. Disruption of either can produce grotesque distortions of behavior, but in the latter case, if one's impulse toward truth has been interrupted, one seeks out falsehood instead of truth, even going so far as to maintain the falsehood with greater conviction after it's been discredited. Knowing full well that one's hair is brown, one calls it "blond," and the very disparity between the word and the reality becomes a source of elation and power, and above all, feelings of independence vis-à-vis the language centers of the brain.

Done with her exercises, Martha went to the bathroom and returned a moment later with a towel. Mopping her face with one hand, she rested the other on my chest as she sat down on the bed beside me. With my head slightly raised by the pillow, I found myself staring at her hand. The sight of it frightened me. It was as if some half-dead, mangy bird of prey had landed on my chest. For several years she'd been working on her technique for breaking boards, even demonstrating it when her dojo held introductory sessions to attract new students, and her fingers were crooked and slightly discolored by years of practice on the striking board, the purplish swellings at the middle knuckle not unlike a sort of jewelry. Face covered, she spoke into the towel, as much to herself as me.

"God, I never felt so loose. Like my body took over and my mind just watched what was going on. Could you tell?" Sliding the towel beneath her eyes, studying me with half her face concealed, she looked as if she were wearing a surgical mask. "All these years of practice, but sometimes it seems like I've just begun. You do it from habit, automatically, but then suddenly you understand. The roots of your negative energy—that's what you've got to change. All the laziness and distraction, the mindlessness, the selfishness—one straight punch with sincerity, one moment of concentration, one deep breath is all it takes to turn it around. And if you don't do it, you can forget about anything else. Your relationship, your work, it's all empty if your energy is wrong." She leaned over and kissed me on the forehead. "Forget what I said before, okay? It was my negativity I was talking about, nothing to do with you. I know where the problem is. It's bullshit to blame it on our marriage."

While she was talking, I looked out the window. For the first time I noticed that it was snowing. Huge flakes drifted back and forth so slowly and haphazardly that as many seemed to rise as fall. The window became a landscape, a dream-landscape, and Martha's voice disappeared within it. Suddenly peaceful, I watched the snowflakes as if I were one of them, as if I were drifting back and forth with the same easy grace. And then all at once a great clarity came upon me, the diagnosis I'd been searching for. I don't know what happened to the arguments and distinctions that had collected around the question of my condition, but suddenly, happily, I thought, "Come off it. This is brain damage, and you know it." Not many words, and certainly nothing that hadn't occurred to me before, but neurologically speaking, the effect of this conclusion was almost like an epileptic seizure. Waves of excitation spread through my brain until it seemed to me that every cell was firing. All the voices disappeared, all confusion fell away. I felt as if my feet were back on the ground, my eyes wide open, the whole world illuminated before me. "This is brain damage and you know it!" The power of language had never been so clear to me. That words originating in one group of cells could excite so many others—did anything we knew about the brain, anything in its chemistry or physiology, explain such miraculous transformation?

"Hey," Martha said, "what's going on? Are you paralyzed or something? You haven't moved since you woke up."

I laughed. "It's nothing," I said. "I'm just thinking. Trying to figure it out."

"Figure what out?"

"Lots of things. I'll tell you later."

"What's that?" she said, touching my cheek. "Are you crying?"

"No," I said, meaning "yes."

CHAPTER FOUR

Confusion ensued, great waves moving to and fro in my brain, as if every firing produced a firing that opposed it. I told myself that I enjoyed it, but since that firing was opposed no less than any other, I told myself a moment later that I didn't. When Martha went back to the roof, I called it "the bathroom," and when mother, trying to help me, suggested that "bathroom" was intentional, a means by which I sought to perpetuate the "myth" of my brain damage, I made no move in the direction of "roof" though I believed her to be correct.

Since I believed it to be an auditory hallucination, the sound of Martha's bathwater terrified me. Gazing out the window, I tried to re-enter the dream of the snowflakes, reconstruct the tranquility which, by this time, in my distorted memory, had been exaggerated beyond recognition. Bliss, it was, and completely unattainable. And since it refused to be replicated, the memory became unbearable, one more source of frustration and disappointment. What creates more symptoms in the brain than memories of bliss?

Father said: "Leaves them that is to say, some find

encouragement in telling him had always been who would not, given the choice, see himself as perverse or indolent instead of paralyzed?"

Unlike mother, who found it "irresponsible," I took his babble as a warning. He was demonstrating, it seemed to me, the value of coherent speech and the danger of its opposite. To be specific: if I continued in the direction I was headed, I would end up sounding like him.

At last a message unopposed! Part of my brain was suddenly angry and astonished. Like a general rallying his troops, it scanned the lethargic cells around it and cried, "Dammit, get moving! Enough is enough!" I realized that my problem was not confusion but infatuation with it, a great desire to push my brain to the end of its tolerance. Anonymous voices shouted, a great chorus of inspirational phrases like "It's now or never!" and "Shit or get off the pot!"

Where else would I turn, at such a moment, except to my most recent anchor, the last of my coherent thoughts—"This is brain damage and you know it!" And what hope I felt as I did so! Never mind that the implications of the thought were negative. From my point of view, thought had independent value. Good or bad, it proved that one's brain was functioning. Even better, one could use the thought to *exercise* the brain, supporting it with evidence, synonyms, particular examples, etc., marshalling more and more cells in its behalf until finally it would cease to be mere opinion and become a "conclusion" or even a "fact." That's what the brain thrives on, isn't it—the invention of "facts" and "conclusions."

Imagine my surprise when I found, not the thought I had remembered, but its opposite! Not five minutes before I had told myself, "This is brain damage and you know it," but now, seeking the thought again, I found instead a voice that asserted, with no less authority than the one it had displaced, "This is not brain damage and you know it."

As if all of my symptoms weren't enough—having my thoughts infiltrated by voices other than my own, saying "bathroom" when I meant "roof" or "roof" when I meant "bathroom" while claiming, in either case, that my mistake had been intentional, ignoring my mother's intelligence while heeding my father's babble—as if all this weren't enough, my brain denied me the one thing that would have given me hope, the ability to confront my disease and describe it with conviction: "This is brain damage and you know it."

God, the power of language! Only the brain-damaged truly appreciate it! How could I know what it meant to say, "I have brain damage" until I found myself unable to? How many times had I seen it confirmed in my office that a man who could say of himself, "I have amnesia," assumed a subtle power over his memory which, though it might not increase the amount of information he recalled, certainly enhanced his hope for doing so or diminished his disappointment if, in spite of all his efforts, his past remained inaccessible to him?

But notice, please, that the emphasis here is less on health than on cooperation. Description is a communal act, not one instrument performing a solo, but a trained and practiced orchestra producing unified sound. A man with amnesia who does not believe that he has amnesia will derive as much benefit from saying "I do not have amnesia" as the man without amnesia, who believes himself to be amnesic, will derive from saying, "I have amnesia." The brain may be playful when it comes to description, but the games it plays are explicit in their rules. A man with amnesia who says of himself, "I have leprosy," will derive the same benefit as another man who says "I have amnesia," simply because, for the former, "leprosy" *means* "amnesia." And even if "leprosy" *means* "leprosy," he may still find happiness in his thought because he believes his failure of memory to be a skin disorder.

Finally, too, there are patients whose problem does not reside in either language or meaning but in the regions that confirm or deny them, those particular clusters of cells in which, when a word or thought "rings a bell," the sound has occurred. Dysfunction in these regions produces chaos in the area of confirmation itself. Such patients hear the bell when they shouldn't or fail to hear it when they should. Even though correct, "This is brain damage" will leave them bereft, and even though incorrect, "This is not brain damage," will produce the sound for which they yearn.

Though I was thinking hard on the matter, I could not locate my symptoms in this picture. I knew I had

the words "brain damage," and it seemed to me I had
the meaning. Furthermore, I had complete confidence
in the system on which I relied for confirmation, the
voice that cried "Yes!" in my brain, the cells that rang
the bell, and those that heard it. Why then, with all of
these functions operating, did I deny myself the description I wanted? Why could I not say of myself, "This
is brain damage"? I was completely baffled until mother
pointed out what ought to have been obvious from the
start—namely, that my first description had been confirmed by the very fact that my second contradicted it.
If one were truly suffering from brain damage, why on
earth would we expect him to be consistent? Who knew
better than I that the essence of brain damage is discontinuity? I'd never known a patient who could make
up his mind and stick to it! To maintain opinions in-
definitely, resisting argument, circumstance, the weak-
ening influence of time itself, or even a point of view
with greater wisdom than one's own—that's the mark
of a healthy brain! The fact that I had reversed myself
was absolute proof that I hadn't!

Thus when Marjorie returned from her bath, I was
whistling aloud. Either "Oh Susannah!" or "Home on
the Range," I didn't know which. Neither mother nor
father had been impressed by my argument, but that,
of course, made it all the more impressive to me. Not
that I was ignoring them—quite the opposite! Each of
their objections made me doubt myself a little more.
But once you've set your sights on contradiction, how
can doubt discourage you? The way I saw it, being

uncertain and being correct were virtually identical. Besides, if my goals were truly scientific, if my ultimate purpose was understanding the brain, how could I feel anything but proud of the discoveries I had made? In addition to everything else I'd learned, it was now becoming clear that, even in the direst straits, wracked with disappointment, confusion and discontinuity, the brain was capable of secreting the whole range of positive emotion—confidence, pride, optimism, even (unless I read it wrong) euphoria. Why else, in the midst of such nightmare, was I whistling aloud? How could I despair over a condition that revealed such secrets? How except through brain damage could one discover the complexities of this organ, the resilience, the incredible duplicity?

"What's that song?" Marjorie said.

" 'Silent Night.' "

"No, it isn't. It's, uh, wait a minute, one of those shmaltz songs, junk music. Mantovani plays it, or maybe Nelson Riddle. Some sort of Christmas song, I know that. Wait, I'll get it in a second."

Naked, she had a towel around her hair like a turban. A short, slender woman, have I said that before? her every movement quick and purposeful, her skin so dark she always seemed to have a tan. Small breasts round and plump as persimmons, at thirty-five the body of a teenager. Convinced I'd never seen her before, I was stunned and thrilled by the sight of her, my erection sudden and heated, almost explosive, forming a mound in the blanket.

" 'Winter Wonderland'!" she cried.

"Who are you?" I said.

"Come on, Drogin," she sighed. "It's too early for that. Ask me after my meditation."

"Come here."

"At least something's moving," she said. "What's that under the blanket?"

"Come here."

"What for?"

"You know what for."

"What about the brain damage?"

"What brain damage?"

"Didn't you say you've got brain damage?"

"Come off it. This is not brain damage, and you know it."

She sat down on the edge of the bed. My hard-on was gone. I knew who she was, and she was not in the least attractive to me.

"What do you want?" I said.

"Nothing," she said. "What do you want?"

"Nothing."

"Fine with me," she snapped, and then, her face reddening, "No, it isn't. What do you think I am, a yo-yo?"

Despite the fact that I did not know what it meant, the word "yo-yo" elicited feelings of melancoly and nostalgia. I repeated it several times to myself, but it remained at once elusive and familiar, like a word in a foreign language that slightly resembled one in my own. All I got was a visual image, something long and thin like a fishing rod. Was it possible that "yo-yo" meant "fishing rod"?

"No, no, Christ almighty," father said. "No nonsense tell you for sure not that a fishing rod."

Martha got up and went to the closet. When she was angry, as now, her lips curled inward, as if she were gritting her teeth behind them. It was an expression I loved when I loved her but found childish and spoiled when I didn't. This time it pierced me like an arrow. Without knowing why, I felt ashamed of myself, unworthy of her, and I resolved with a great thrust to sit up, drink my coffee, give up what mother called "this brain-damage nonsense," and have a normal conversation beginning with "I love you."

As if to reinforce my decision, I put my finger high up in my nose. I'm not altogether sure of it, but I believe I had the conviction or at least the hope that as long as I kept my finger there my brain would be inactive.

"Do you want a tissue?" Martha snapped.

"No thanks."

"Come here, go away. Once a surgeon, always a surgeon. Everything's a power trip with him. Give it up, Drogin! Leave it in the operating room!" There was a small striking board mounted on the wall opposite the bed, and she hit it twice with each hand. Though it was mounted on foam rubber to protect the wall and deaden the noise, the room shook with each punch. The sounds were explosive but muted, like thunder in the distance or a butcher pounding meat.

She was talking to herself. "And every time I fall for

it! Total fucking masochist. I don't even feel like sex but I'm sitting on the bed while he makes up his mind! Do I need this? Tell me that, will you? How can you do karate if he's jerking your head around?" She closed her eyes and rubbed them with her fingers, then suddenly turned to me laughing. "Tell me the truth, okay, honey? Did you want to fuck just then? I know I didn't. Sex was the last thing on my mind."

She waited for me to answer and when I didn't, a look of concern spread over her face, as if she'd only now become aware of my paralysis. "Hey, what's wrong? Tell me, okay?"

"I love you."

"So? What's wrong with that?"

"What's wrong with that?" I said. "What do you think I am, a yo-yo?"

"Yo-yo?" Her eyes closed, and then she opened one. It was the same look I'd seen earlier, as if she were gazing at me along the barrel of a gun. "Honey, please don't mess around, okay? Tell me what's going on."

I lifted my hands in front of my face, cupping them slightly, as if gripping an imaginary basketball. A gesture like that, measured and controlled, gentle but not without authority—no way you could doubt the brain of a man that made it.

"Stick with me!" I cried. "I'm very close!"

"Close to what?"

I dropped one hand but not the other. It seemed to me that I had answered her, but from the look on her face, I could tell I hadn't. I could see her thinking while she waited for more. Our eyes were fixed on each other, my right hand suspended before me, palm out now, as if to cry "Halt!" like a traffic copy.

"As you like," she said at last. "You know you don't have to explain yourself to me."

She opened the closet and took out her meditation robe and stepped into it, pulling it over her shoulders and tying the thin rope-like cord that served as its belt. It was a beige, floor-length robe made especially for her by a fellow karate student, a professional seamstress who was also a Black Belt. Martha had been practicing sitting meditation since her days in India. She worked part time these days, having cut back so as to devote herself to karate, but even when a full-time nurse she'd kept the same meditation schedule: forty-five minutes every morning and a half-hour before dinner in the evening. Since her karate teacher—a man they called "Sensei"—believed that meditation was essential to the martial arts, he held regular sessions at the school as well—two-hour periods three evenings a week and one day a month when all the students sat together from five in the morning till nine at night.

One of the rooms in our apartment had been set aside for her meditation. It was a windowless cubicle, not much more than eight feet square, and there was nothing in it but a pair of black cushions—a small round one on a large rectangular one—a shelf where she kept her books on Zen, Yoga, karate, etc., and an altar similar to the one she'd set up in our bedroom, with a vase and a water bowl and a wooden Japanese Buddha. On one wall hung pictures of Sensei and her first meditation instructor, a Tibetan lama with whom she'd studied six months while living in Kathmandu.

She was twenty years old at that time. She'd quit college and taken a job with a relief agency, working in Tibetan refugee camps on the Indian border. During four years in India and Nepal, she'd studied Yoga, Tibetan Buddhism and Vedanta and had lived for five months at an ashram run by one of those freelance gurus who could now be seen on cable television.

Tending the sick in the refugee camps had led her, when she returned to the States, to enter nursing school, and that's how we met, three years later, when she was twenty-six and I was thirty-five and we worked at the same hospital. At that time, as now, she considered herself a hypocrite and a failure. Her time in India, she said, had been completely wasted. She'd learned nothing there except how "rigid" and "insincere" she was. All the great teachings had been presented to her, but not a trace had penetrated the dull thickness of her "clinging" mind. "As far as I can see," she told me, "I'm not one iota less deluded, not one iota less enslaved to my ego."

It wasn't all that difficult to convince myself that it was my shortcoming, not hers, which made such language sound like gibberish. Besides, the truth of the matter was that I never loved her so much as when she spoke in a manner I could not understand. We'd never spent much time together, but when we did, I'd always tried my best to be compatible with her. For a short time, in the early days of our marriage, I had even meditated with her. Two or three months, as I recall. Both of us knew it was useless, but she begged me to try, so I did. I found no objection to it. It just seemed redundant after neurosurgery, sort of thin beside what happened in the operating room—interrupting what was necessary in order to remind you what was necessary. Like when they woke patients in the hospital in order to give them sleeping pills.

Martha said I was narrow-minded, attached to a limited, materialistic point of view, believed in appearances, was stuck in "the Relative World," oblivious to the "Absolute." I asked her what she meant by "Absolute," and she said, "The essential, the enduring, that which is beyond time and space, beyond matter, beyond the flesh. That which is never born and never dies." She was totally sincere, not just religious but a bit of a fanatic. The way she saw it, my mind was in the dark. Heathen, banal, addicted to information, "drowning in phenomena." She didn't blame me, she said, and she didn't love me any less. It was just something we'd have to live with.

Since I felt more or less the same about myself as she did, agreed with her that I was limited and narrow-minded—how could I not be, when I spent twelve to fourteen hours a day at the hospital and never read a book or a newspaper or anything else that didn't relate to my work—there was really no argument between us. We just agreed, as they say, to disagree, and after that, meditation was never mentioned in the house. If it drove us apart, I wasn't aware of it. I was always happy to know that she was in the meditation room. It's true I was also happy to know that I wasn't in there with her, but that was my problem, not hers. I'd never heard a conversation on religion in which both people didn't end up more confused than when they started, so as far as I was concerned, we were lucky to get it out of the way.

When Martha returned from her meditation, half an hour later, her face was radiant. Sitting down on the edge of the bed, she reached under the blanket and found my hand, then sat for awhile, squeezing it gently. Her voice when she finally spoke was a kind of hoarse whisper, very deep but shaky and tentative, with long pauses between words, as if she'd planned what she wanted to say and then forgotten it. I want to say it was a different voice, not at all like the one with which I was familiar, but given my memory problems, which made almost everything unfamiliar, how can I trust that sort of description?

"I don't know how to say this," she said, "but I feel like something *intense* is going on. *Really intense.* Stop me if you want. I don't want to make you self-conscious or anything, but while I was sitting, I got to some things I've never seen before. Total clarity, silence, as if time stopped, as if every illusion fell away. Listen, you know I'm an old hand at this. I've been sitting for what? Eleven years? Twelve? I've been through all the traps, all the trances, the ecstacy, all the bullshit fantasies. I don't want to romanticize this. I'm not saying it's the

end of the world. No great enlightenment, just vibes of
a sort I've never known. It wasn't even pleasant! It was
very uncomfortable, even painful. Like everything was
crumbling underneath me. Like pure emptiness, you
know, the sort of thing you read about in the sutras
but never experience on your own. I can't explain it
but my guess is it's coming from you. What do you
think, honey? Am I imagining this? Tell me if I'm crazy!"

Truthfully, I didn't follow her. I wanted to, but I
couldn't. And it seemed to me that this particular con-
junction, wanting and failing to pay attention, was the
essence of my dysfunction. My attention was there, but
the wanting had sabotaged it, as if certain cells were
ready and willing to concentrate, but certain others had
interfered with them. The effort to concentrate, in other
words, had ruined my concentration!

"What's a yo-yo?" I said.

"A yo-yo? Well, it's a sort of—" Marjorie caught
herself, smiling. "Okay, I get the point. No trespassing,
right? Keep off the grass. I don't blame you. If I were
into what you're into, I wouldn't want someone looking
over my shoulder either."

She went to the closet and took off her robe, then
slipped on some jeans and a sweatshirt and a pair of
long red winter socks. Rummaging in the dresser drawer,
she took out a green woolen cap and adjusted it carefully
while looking in the mirror. She put a down vest over
her sweatshirt and a red-and-black plaid jacket over
the vest, and then she went out in the hall to get her
boots. A moment later, with knee-high boots laced up

outside her jeans, she stood in the bedroom door. "I'm going to the dojo for a while. Do you need anything? Will you be all right without me?"

Framed by the doorway, thick with all her winter clothes, she looked unfamiliar again. Almost shockingly beautiful. I felt sad, then angry at the thought of her going, then very frightened at being alone. The impulse was strong to take her into my confidence. It seemed that if I could explain myself to anyone, it was her. And that if anything would appease my brain, it was explanation. Every organ has its favorite nutrients, and the brain's are reason and logic, anything that justifies its methods, shores up its power. Is it any wonder I was so attracted to incoherence? If I allowed such explanation, if by chance I were able to define and understand my project, I would erase all the progress I had made, kill my chances, whatever they were, of investigating whatever it was I wanted to investigate. I didn't yet know that what kept me going was not knowing where I was headed, but even so, I turned away instinctively from any thought that promised knowledge.

So a great battle raged within me, certain cells begging for coherence, others for its opposite, and neither had the faintest idea what I was up to. A great smile spread over my face, and I took up the basketball again. I dropped one hand, then opened and closed the other six or seven times. In other words, I was waving at Martha as if I were a two-year-old. With a feeling of intimacy, love beyond any I'd ever known for her, and a clearcut, single-minded decision in favor of incoherence, I said, "Brain damage? Why not?"

"Hunh?" She seemed stunned for a moment, almost as if I'd struck her, but then, shaking her head in disbelief, her voice just barely a whisper, she smiled as only someone can who doesn't feel like smiling. "Yeah!" sho said. "Why not?"

Chapter Five

As I've mentioned, father had sometimes taken me with him to his operating room, and it was there I found him when Martha shut the door behind her. It was a different sort of room from the one we used, much smaller and simpler, with less technology in evidence. A large window overlooked a garden below, and the instrument stand was not, as in our rooms, above the table, but beside it so that his tools were always visible and if he liked, he could reach for them himself. There was no microscope, of course, no video equipment, no oscilloscope on the wall, and the overhead lights were not too much bigger than those you'd find in a modern kitchen.

Father was vague in the room at first, but gradually I realized he was operating, and that the patient on the table was me. It was not so unusual for someone with brain damage to have this sort of fantasy. I'd had many patients who imagined themselves on the operating table. There were five or six observers in the room, and despite the fact that they were wearing masks, I recognized both mother and Eli among them. Father ex-

plained that the purpose of the operation was to "cat-
alogue his symptoms and arrive at their source so as,
if possible, to eliminate them once and for all." What
he wanted to locate especially, he said, were the cells
that had produced my most recent problem, the motor
dysfunction indicated by my paralysis. He wanted to
demonstrate that it was not, as I had contended, a matter
of volition. If I had actually *decided* not to move, my
problem would be located in my Frontal Lobes, but he
would show that it was in fact derived from cells in
my Motor Region, with some assistance from those
adjacent to them that were involved with language. In
other words, however much I claimed that I had chosen
not to move, the truth of the matter was that I couldn't,
even if I wanted to. What we had here, he said, was
a fascinating syndrome. He wanted to map the neurology
of the belief-system that caused me to think I'd chosen
my condition. As he saw it, it was typical of patients
like myself, helpless before our brains, to imagine ourselves in control of them. One particular circuit in the
brain produced such fantasy, visions of omnipotence
and absolute control, dreams of a self or soul beyond
the brain that was capable of manipulating it. If this
operation succeeded, he said, he would identify that
circuit and eliminate it, thus helping me, finally, to
accept my brain's control over every aspect of my life.

To my disappointment, the surgery never progressed
beyond this point. Mother and Eli joined in the dis-
cussion, but most comments, including father's, were
repeated three or four times with no word changed,

and the mapping procedure never began. I saw and heard the same scenario, again and again, until Martha returned. In fact, the entire hallucination reminded me of those I'd produced, in patients like Lucinda, on the operating table. Like theirs, it was circular and self-duplicating, extremely convincing on the one hand but vague and unresolved on the other. Always the same, always at the same pace, it began and ended like a film clip, terminating abruptly, then beginning again where it had before, as if the cells in which the fantasy were stored had no capacity to alter or expand it.

With patients on the operating table, the information disappeared when the electrode was deactivated. In my case, it disappeared when I heard Martha's key in the door. From that instant, the operating room disappeared and the conversation in it ceased. I was back in the world which, though it was much less real at the moment than the one I'd left behind, my brain called "reality."

One of the pleasures of brain damage is that you don't have to do anything. Since nothing's expected of you, you can't disappoint people or make them angry. In fact, most people treat you as if you're blind and deaf, exaggerating your incapacities, as if their brains cannot conceive that you have any brain at all. It's harder for them to fathom a less-than-perfect brain than no brain at all.

So it was with Martha now. "Honey, I've brought Sensei," she said, as if I couldn't see for myself. And then, speaking to Sensei as if I couldn't hear what she was saying, "That's just the way I left him. He hasn't moved an inch. Head propped at that same uncomfortable angle on the pillow, the same glazed look in his eye, the same fixed, exaggerated smile." Then she turned to me again, yelling now, as if I weren't quite deaf but simply hard of hearing, "DROGIN! I'VE BROUGHT SENSEI! YOU REMEMBER SENSEI, DON'T YOU?"

Sensei placed his palms together and bowed to me, then sat down on the end of the bed and folded his legs into the Lotus position. He was barefoot, wearing black pants and an orange velvet shirt that hung almost to his knees. Eyes closed, pursing his lips in concentration, he took a deep breath and held it. He seemed to be trying to figure something out or to rid his brain of troubling thought, but then suddenly he exhaled, smiling happily, as if he'd done what he had to do or found what he was looking for. Each foot rested sole-up on the opposite thigh and his hands were cupped in his lap. I noticed that his fingers, from practice on the striking board, were even more swollen and discolored than Martha's.

"What do you think?" she said.

"I see what you mean about the vibrations," he said. "The light in this room is extremely clear. Not a trace of negative energy!"

He must have been six-four or five, a wiry man with a shaved, pointed head and huge ears that stood away from it like cups. Whatever ideas one had about a Master of the Martial Arts, he contradicted them absolutely.

His small brown eyes were mournful as a dog's. Though somewhere in his mid-forties, he looked to be nearly sixty. There were deep lines in his forehead and around his mouth, dark circles of thickened skin beneath his eyes. As our eyes met now, I was very disappointed to find that I remembered him.

Why disappointed? Because certain regions of my brain remained fascinated with my deficits. Especially amnesia. In these regions it seemed a great shame that there was more to this man than I saw before me, that my memory should present me with information concerning his past, conversations between us, conversations between Martha and me regarding him, etc. Knowing him, recognizing him, connecting what he was to what he had been, all the neurology in short that leads to social behavior, relationship, continuity, time outside the present—to me it seemed degenerative, threatening, even pathological. We are already aware of my brain's tendency to glorify amnesia, but I suspect that the real symptom here was the belief that, if I could liberate myself from memory, I could liberate myself from the past in general and therefore time itself. It was almost as if, by remembering this man, I had lost a chance for perfect liberation, as if the gateway to timelessness and immortality had opened before me, and I had turned my back on it.

Martha had often invited him to eat with us, and when he came he usually stayed late, talking with me after she had gone to bed. His name, I believe, was Frank Rush, or Fred, and he considered himself a teacher of meditation as well as karate. He called me his colleague because he believed that he too was a sort of physician, having been born with an extraordinary capacity for psychic healing. The effect of his "treatments," he said, was a purification of mind and body that defied logic and surpassed by many levels the achievements of modern medicine. Among the diseases he had cured he listed angina pectoris, Parkinson's disease, multiple sclerosis, ulcers, Hodgkin's disease and other cancers, migraine headaches, low-back syndrome, arthritis, and a whole range of psychological problems that included paranoia, manic-depression, obsessive-compulsive disorders, phobias of every sort, and a generalized problem that he called "negativity."

"There is no one I can refuse as a patient," he told me, "and very, very few who do not need my help. Why? Because negative energy is universal. A result of the ignorance and delusion that are the inescapable consequence of being born. No one is undeluded except the truly Enlightened, and in case you haven't noticed, such people are not in great supply at the present time. If you want my honest opinion, the only people who do not ask for my help are those who, because of the very problems for which they need me, are unaware of them."

Much as Marjorie had talked about them, I was never able to visualize what actually happened during Fred's treatments until I saw for myself. After scrutinizing me for several minutes, he asked Martha to leave the room so that he and I could be alone. As soon as she was

gone, he kneeled beside me and placed one hand on
the middle of my chest, the other on a point just below
my navel. Closing his eyes, he breathed deeply, held
his breath for what must have been thirty or forty
seconds, and then expelled it very slowly. Then he was
silent for maybe five minutes, moving his fingers ever
so slightly and pressing them gently into my skin until
he shook his head in what seemed a kind of amazement.

"You're not fooling around, are you?" he said. "Turn
over!"

When I didn't move, he slipped one hand under my
shoulders, the other under my hips, and turned me
himself. Another silence followed. Five more minutes.
He kept one hand on the small of my back, the other
between my shoulder blades. Finally, he exhaled loudly,
turned me on my back again and, after pulling me up
into a sitting position, climbed onto my chest.

Breathing heavily, he stared into my eyes for nearly
five minutes. There was rage in his eyes, a kind of
desperation, as if he wanted to penetrate my eyes and
see what lay behind them. Then suddenly he grabbed
my head and lifted it off the pillow and rocked it from
side to side, crying, "Feel my fingers! Listen to them!
Yes! That's it! Keep going! No separation! See it, Isaac!
See it! There's no separation between us! Your head,
my hands! My head, your head. My brain, your brain!
No separation!"

Perspiration beaded on his forehead. I felt his breath
like a breeze on my face and smelled its slightly pungent
odor. Until this moment, "energizing" had had no effect

on me, but now, as I felt his fingers on my skull, it struck me like a thunderbolt that they were very *close to my brain*. In fact, the middle and ring fingers of his right hand were less than two inches from the Left Cerebral region in which, as I understood it, the vision of father's operating room had taken shape.

The response to these thoughts was immediate and volatile. Waving his hands and circling the table, father became aggressive and hysterical, flooding my brain with an incomprehensible tirade of medical and surgical terms. "Arachnoid!" he cried. "Why not? I'd say anisocoria too. Nystagmus in all directions! Acoustic neuroma growing toward the pons. Aphasia! Anoxia! Agraphia! Right bilateral papilledema!"

What was strange was that the more incoherent he became, the less he bothered me. Indeed, after trying in vain to follow him, I realized that he had liberated me, not only from his own voice, but also from every other sound my brain was making. In a flash, I had my confidence back. (Is that self-confidence then? Freedom from the need to pay attention to your brain?) No longer "an illness," brain damage was simply the clearest and most direct route to the Truth that lay beyond neurology. You could say that I had now begun to see my brain as an endless source of fabrication. Lying was its business, while I wanted Truth. Memory was its business, but I wanted freedom from the past. Finally, "coherence" was its business, its ultimate trap, but I wanted chaos and confusion of the sort that father, in all his wisdom and kindness, was lavishing on me now.

Yes, I thought, everything is clear! Only when the brain malfunctions can you see how much it hurts you when it doesn't. Only then can you see how it connects one moment to another. This Frank for instance to yesterday's Frank, tomorrow's Drogin to today's, the opinion I held a moment ago to the one I hold now, etc. That's what you call correct neurological function! But in brain damage, I saw, all that disappears. Only *this moment* exists. Frank has no past, and I have no opinion except the one to which I'm committed now. There's no such thing as change because there's nothing to change from. There's no such thing as death because there's no such thing as time. Who, having experienced this sort of freedom, could feel anything but gratitude at signs that his brain is disintegrating? And who, when struck with fear at signs of such disintegration, could fail to see that such fear was nothing more than the last vestige of correct neurological function acting in its own defense?

I don't deny that I doubted these thoughts, but once again, I took my doubt as proof of their validity. I knew that something of great value was happening and that with just a little effort I'd get at what it was . . . but of course that was precisely what I did not want to do. To "get" at it would be to comprehend it, and what was comprehension but knowledge and memory, in other words, neurological information, all sorts of co-ordinated discharge and secretion that would strengthen my brain instead of helping me escape it. More than ever, I was determined not to let this happen. So much

so that as soon as I realized this—that I was determined
not to let this happen—I forgot it. I can honestly say
that at that moment I did not know where I was, where
I'd been, where I hoped to be or, finally, what I meant
to accomplish by means of my confusion.

Still gripping my head, Frank's voice was thick with
emotion. "Isaac!" he cried. "What are you feeling?"

Fixed and unblinking, his eyes seemod bigger and
brighter, nothing like the sad, dull eyes I'd seen before.
It was almost as if these orbs that sent information to
his brain were now receiving information from within,
which increased the amount of light that they themselves emitted. A tremor caused his lower lip to vibrate.
For several minutes he continued squeezing my head,
then finally he lowered it gently to the pillow. He was
breathless.

"What are you feeling?" he said again.

Sliding off the bed, he stood above me for a moment,
gazing down with what seemed a forced severity. He
seemed uneasy with his uneasiness, as if he were thinking more than he meant to at this particular moment
and was looking for me, by answering him, to make
his thinking stop. Exercising like an athlete, he shook
his fingers and rolled his shoulders forward and back
and snapped his head from side to side as if to work
out a kink in his neck.

Then suddenly his eyes narrowed, and his face took
on a happy expression. "That's rare energy, my friend.
Absolutely transparent. I've never seen the likes of it
before. Oh, you know what I'm talking about! You can't

fool me! Your smile tells me everything! This is a golden opportunity, and I'm gonna see that you make the best of it. We'll work together! Break the resistance, take it all the way! But let's go slow, okay? That's enough for today. I don't want to tire you. I'll come back tomorrow, and we'll pick it up where we left off."

Standing in the doorway, he placed his palms together and bowed to me again. "Be brave," he whispered. "With that sort of energy, you've nothing to fear! Just remember, what you're doing is not for you alone. All mankind, the whole universe, will benefit if you can see it through!"

CHAPTER SIX

Unfortunately, while I was regaining my confidence, Martha was losing hers. The fear that I was seriously ill had finally taken hold of her. "What do you think?" she asked Frank. "Should we call an ambulance?"

She was serving him tea, as she often did, in front of the altar at the opposite side of the bedroom. Not ordinary tea. This was Japanese powdered tea that she had learned to prepare in the formal manner, in a special three-month course conducted by a visiting Japanese Master of Tea Ceremony. Except for myself and Frank, and maybe one or two other people, she never offered anyone else this tea, which was very expensive and imported from Japan, and she never served it anywhere but here, at the altar in the bedroom. Facing each other on the orange carpet, they sat back on their heels, two yellow porcelain bowls on a small tea-cloth she'd spread out between them. After portioning out the tea with a wooden spoon, she added water from a small black iron kettle and then stirred it with a bamboo wisk which, like the bowls, the kettle and the wooden spoon, she never used except for this particular ceremony.

Frank took his tea and bowed to her as he'd bowed
to me, and then, cupping it gently, closed his eyes and
breathed its aroma. "An ambulance? Do I hear you
correctly?"

"You know you do, Sensei. Something's going on with
him, and I don't like it. It's all very well to talk about
energy, but dammit, I'm a nurse! I've seen anuerysms,
strokes, epilepsy, a whole lot of stuff that could mess
him up like this. If he's got something like that, if we
sit here calling it 'spiritual' when he's in desperate need
of treatment, we could be wasting valuable time, sac-
rificing him to some private romantic idea that's all
about us and nothing to do with him."

Frank emptied his bowl in a single swallow, tilting
it until it nearly covered his face. Watching him drink,
I could not help remembering, with no little envy, the
amount of caffeine that tea of this sort contained. Prepared from leaves of the first spring growth and ground
to the finest powder, it was two or three times as potent
as ordinary leaf-tea brewed in the English manner.
Though Martha contended that its effects were "spiritual" while the effects of coffee were "sensual," that
it "centered" you and helped your concentration while
coffee, increasing the speed and quantity of your
thoughts, did the opposite, I had never seen a difference
between them. The jolt I got from one was like the jolt
I got from the other, and given my present condition,
with father continuing his tirade and mother and Eli
joining in, I would have given up all my research for
a bit of either circulating in my brain. That's how the

brain tricks you, of course, with smaller pleasures that
turn you away from the larger ones, but at that moment,
thanks to another of its tricks, I'd forgotten what the
larger pleasure was.

Frank put a finger on his ear. "Did I hear you correctly?" he said again. "I think my ears are playing
tricks on me."

"Oh come on, Sensei. Look at his eyes! Totally vacant,
not a sign of recognition there! I've seen eyes like that!
Tumor patients can look like that, or people with leaking
anuerysms. Even epileptics. Sometimes, even when they
haven't had a seizure, you'll see that same void in their
eyes, as if life's been drained from them with only a
shred of consciousness remaining to tell them what's
been lost. You know what we call brain damage in the
hospital? 'Super Death'! Because it's the only death you
stay alive to witness!"

Done with her tea, she placed her bowl in front of
her and bowed with palms together. Then she washed
the bowls and brush with boiling water, stirring with
the wisk as she'd stirred the tea.

Frank waited till she was done before he answered
her. " 'Super Death'? I like the sound of that! 'Super
Death' is everywhere, isn't it? Listen: how many people
have you known who could truly be called 'alive'? Sure,
they're conscious and walking around, but what do they
see? What do they feel? They're attached to their
thoughts, trapped in their paranoia. Confused, frightened, selfish, filled with negativity—if that's not death,
what is?"

"Sure, I know that," Martha said, "but this is different, Sensei. When you're dealing with disease, you're in a different . . . well, a different . . . sure, I know what you're talking about, and you know I agree with you, but—"

When talking with Frank, she sometimes stammered like this, as if two different sound-tracks were running through her brain. Even with subjects on which she was knowledgable, she had difficulty disagreeing with him. But since she couldn't forget or deny what she knew, she tried to say it and not-say it at the same time. The result was that in his presence she seemed timid and younger, a teenager in fact, with maybe 70 percent of her normal intelligence.

But while all of this was going on, I could also see the caffeine take effect. You don't have to be a neurologist to know when someone's mood is improving. Her voice grew stronger, and the fear and tension disappeared from her face. Soon her desire to agree with him had neurochemical support. However much she feared for my condition, her brain was secreting information to the contrary. With spirits soaring, and Frank encouraging them, it wouldn't be long before her pessimism struck her as cowardice.

Frank spoke in a reverential tone. "Have you ever read The Tibetan Book of the Dead"?

"Of course."

"Well, what do you think, that it's only meant for ritual? That it only applies to reincarnation? Don't you know that we're all of us living and dying all the time?

Listen, Martha: every moment is a lifetime! Every moment each of us is reincarnated! That means we're
always crossing the river between lifetimes, passing
through what Tibetans call the 'Bardo.' Anyone who
grows, who really transforms between one moment and
the next, he has to go through the Bardo just as someone
does when he dies. How can you find yourself if you
aren't willing to lose yourself? How can you change
without relinquishing what you were? Don't you see,
Marcia? Your husband is in the Bardo! Forget 'Super
Death'! This man is dead! Crossing the river! He's between lifetimes! His soul is wandering! Every demon in
the universe is fighting to possess it! There's no pre-
dicting where he'll end up, and there's nothing we can
do to help him. He's on his own! All we can do is be
here when he needs us, and of course, make sure we
don't interfere. And nothing would interfere like a doctor. Doctors hate the Bardo! They'd sooner kill a soul
than let it wander!"

To say the least, 'Marcia' caught me by surprise.
Despite the fact that 'Martha' had never really convinced me, I'd begun to grow comfortable with it, which
is to say that it now elicited very little secondary comment in my brain. Isn't that the mark of truth, neurologically speaking, when the product of one cluster
of cells evokes no dissent from others? Now I had
'Marcia' to deal with, a name I could only doubt by
assuming that their conversation, like the one that had
occurred in father's office, was hallucinatory, that 'Marcia' therefore was no less a product of my dysfunction

than the name it had replaced. If father was right, I
mean, about the extent of my brain damage, and this
conversation was received and processed by means of
the functions he believed to be diseased, why should
I trust Frank's language any more than I trusted my
own?

I know now of course that another possibility exists,
one I could not consider at that time, since it concerns
my memory more than my perception. Since both names,
'Martha' and 'Marcia,' are products of my present memory, aren't they both perhaps to be regarded with suspicion? Isn't it possible that Frank—if that was his
name—did not call her 'Marcia'? Or that, even if he
called her 'Marcia,' Marcia was not her name? Let us
remember that he is remembered too. I don't want to
complicate these matters any more than necessary, but
how can we forget that the brain from which I derive
his memory is also the brain that kept me mute and
paralyzed, frozen in bed while he talked? If the neurology of naming is complex, the neurology of remembered naming is infinitely more so. And when you have
a brain which, seeking to reconstruct the history of its
own disease, is as eager as mine to demonstrate its
freedom from amnesia, how can you trust that all its
memories are not in fact invented? There is no way of
knowing whether I perceived their conversation incorrectly, remember it incorrectly now, or have invented
it altogether so as to exercise the cells from which such
invention is derived and/or encourage those from which

the memories might have been derived, had they not been dysfunctional.

From a neurological point of view, it doesn't matter which of these alternatives apply. If the brain, as I hope, is a self-correcting and self-regenerating organism, the important thing is not what the memory is or used to be but what it will be, in the future. How much will it be credited, how much elaborated, how will it affect my synapses, my metabolism? If comments like these continue, reflection that tends to undermine a simple choice of names, if I can't call my wife 'Marcia' without arousing doubt and self-criticism, we can hardly expect such recollections to speed my convalesence. But if 'Marcia' gathers conviction, if 'Martha' and 'Marjorie' are never heard again, I'll be that much closer to the condition from which, in those days, I longed so much to escape.

While it's obvious from that paragraph, for example, that my thought-process remains in disarray, what's the extent of its debility? Is it waxing or waning, losing support or gaining it among the cells that remain available? In effect, what are we to conclude from the fact that I am losing my concentration now? Is it proof that my incapacity continues or an indication that my improvement, increasing the quantity of my thoughts, has raised questions about my memory that interrupt it? I can't deny that, less healthy, my brain maintained a more consistent point of view, but how can I doubt my neurology when my brain's description of itself continues to be, unless I view it wrongly, so accurate and exhaustive?

"I don't understand!" Marcia cried.

Frank leaned forward, rolling his shoulders as he'd rolled them before. "Well, that's the first step, to admit you don't. Without blame or guilt or apology, to say of yourself: 'I'm ignorant.' To realize that you cannot possibly understand him when you look at him with *Relative Eyes*. Isn't it obvious, Marcia? All you can see is that he's not what he used to be. From that point of view—*relative point of view*—your reaction is totally reasonable! But from the *point of view of the Absolute*, it's completely deluded. Don't you see? This man is not in the Relative World! You are, but he isn't! He embodies everything I teach at the dojo. He's beyond memory, beyond language, beyond dualism, beyond space and time. How can you understand him when you remain attached to such phenomena?" A long silence followed. Lips pursed, eyes so tightly shut that the top of her cheeks nearly touched her eyebrows, Marcia's face was squeezed with conflict, as if she were caught and held suspended between her different points of view.

Frank picked up the kettle and moved it a few inches to the right. "Look," he said, "right now, at this moment, this kettle is located here, right? You say it used to be there, but now it's here, right? You say, 'It's moved, its position has changed,' but how do you know? How do you know it used to be there? What do you mean by 'here' and 'there'? Where do you get the whole concept of movement and change? It's all memory, isn't it? All comparison. That's *Relative Mind* talking, a mind that's attached to appearances, the limited, transient world of phenomena. 'It used to be here, but now it's there.'

"For *Absolute Mind*, that makes no sense. From its point of view, change does not exist. The kettle is always here and always there because, fundamentally speaking, there's no difference between 'here' and 'there.' From a *Relative* point of view, all things are distinct from each other. Here and there, me and you, now and then, subject and object. From an *Absolute* point of view, there's no such distinction. You and I are one, now and then are one, subject and object are one, and finally, disease and health are one. Let Isaac be sick, let him be healthy! From this point of view, it makes no difference at all!

"Oh, I know what you're thinking! 'We live in the Relative World! We eat, we shit, we make love, we make war. We have our bodies, and we have to take care of them!' I don't argue with that. As long as we live in the world of delusion, our delusions must be honored! But what happens when someone begins to relinquish his delusions? What happens when subject and object cease to be separate for him? When 'here' and 'there' are always here? When time dissolves and 'now' endures forever? When life and death are one? If such a man, living on that level, appears amongst us, how can we, who remain deluded, undertake to judge him? No, Marcia, I say we can't. I say that such a man exists in a realm that cannot be fathomed by minds as ignorant and obstructed as ours continue to be. I say

that if we're serious about our practice, if we want to
realize the Absolute within ourselves, all we can do is
bow down to this man. Accept him, without qualifi-
cation, *exactly as he is.*"

Though mother and father and Eli, along with everyone else in the office, agreed that this was "irrational"
and "irresponsible" ("The sort of a monologue," Eli
explained, "that we often hear when brain damage
distorts thought-process but leaves a good deal of language intact"), Marcia found it liberating. By the time
Frank finished, a great smile had appeared on her face
and she was shaking her head with wonder and gratitude. "Oh Jesus!" she cried. "It's all so clear isn't it?
All you have to do is open your eyes!"

"Yes, that's true," Frank replied. "But it's easier said
than done! Very few people have the courage to open
their eyes, Marjorie. When you open your eyes, you let
go of your relative point of view. And most people
prefer to hold onto their relative point of view, even if
it makes them suffer. Even those who've seen the Absolute will often continue to treat it as an enemy."

"But it's all about energy, isn't it? How can you realize
yourself if your energy isn't right? True energy looks
wild or insane or pathological to those whose lives are
attached to false energy! That's what we see in Drogin,
isn't it? True energy! Absolute energy! How can I call
him 'sick' when it's me who's really ill? How can I
question his brain when my own brain is so deluded?
How can I pretend to see him when I've yet to open
my eyes?"

"Exactly. And yet, as a nurse, who knows better than you the pain and confusion and terror that one encounters in periods of transition, trying to make the sort of turn that Isaac, leaving one energy level and moving toward another, is trying to make just now? Calling him 'sick'—isn't that just a way of turning your back on his energy merely because it frightens you?"

"Absolutely!" Millie cried. "Oh God, I've never seen it so well! Energy is freedom! Freedom is the Absolute! And yet we resist! Even when we understand we continue to resist! The door of our prison stands open before us, but we refuse to leave! Why, Sensei? Why? It's almost as if we want to continue suffering! As if we prefer ignorance to understanding, misery to joy! Why?"

"Because your suffering is your ego, Millie. Your ignorance begins and ends with your attachment to Relative Mind. From the point of view of the Absolute, there's no difference between misery and joy, but tell that to your ego! Don't you understand? The ego lives by discrimination! Judgment and attachment, dualism, separation of subject and object. Any vision of the Absolute is death to the ego, the end of its reign of terror."

Frank stood up and sat beside me on the bed again. Martha stood behind him, but he spoke in a whisper, as if he did not want her to hear. "Isaac? Can you hear me? Listen, I don't know if you understood what I was saying, but if you did, I hope you'll forgive it. Where you're at now, you don't need to think about such things. People like us, we're in a different place than you are. We need concepts, ideas, targets we can aim at. What do you need with a target when you're living in the bull's-eye?" He placed his hands on my head again and—closing his eyes, inhaling and holding his breath, then finally exhaling slowly—went through the procedure I'd seen before. After a long silence, he exclaimed with an air of relief, "Well, you're not backing off, are you? Martha! Come here a minute!"

Martha came around to the other side of the bed and sat with her hip against my shoulder. Their weight on either side of me had pulled the sheet and blanket tight around my chest. He took her hands and placed them on my head.

"What do you feel?"

"Well, it's very warm. I feel tremendous heat coming off him."

"Is that all?"

"Yes . . . no . . . wait. I feel a sort of tingling in my fingertips."

"Is that all?"

Again she was silent, staring at the wall above my head. "No, of course not," she said at last. "But there's no way to put it in words."

"Okay!" he said. "I was wondering when you'd get it! Realization like this cannot be articulated. It's beyond language! Beyond the rational mind! From now on, whenever you doubt him, whenever you fear for his health, remember this feeling, Marjorie, the energy in your fingertips. And remember that it's your rational mind that doubts and fears, the mind that he has cast aside. This is the wisdom of karate, Martha, the wisdom of Zen and the wisdom of true energy. What you're holding in your hands is everything I've taught you at the dojo!"

Martha shook her head in agreement, but her eyes were fearful, uncertain, moving back and forth between Frank's and my own. That the desire to agree and the ability to do so were separate and often contradictory neurological functions had not yet occurred to her. Suddenly she stood up and took a step back from the bed, bowed with her palms together, then dropped to her knees and placed her forehead on the floor. Her head remained on the carpet for four or five seconds, and then she stood up and went through it all again. Three times she dropped to her knees and placed her head on floor, and each time, when she stood up, her face showed less doubt. Finally, after three prostrations, there was no doubt at all. Not a trace of uncertainty, not a trace of suspicion, nothing but confidence and conviction. Her face was radiant, almost as if she'd stripped her brain of all its dissident voices, as if she'd unified it by the simple act of turning it upside down.

CHAPTER SEVEN

It's safe to say, I think, that over the last century no neurological function has been investigated more than volition. Experimental lesions in animal brains, pathological lesions (tumors and aneurysms, for example) in human brains, surgery such as that performed by my father and other lobotomists—anything that interferes with the normal activity of will power and intentionality—has been explored and documented with renewed enthusiasm as each new generation of technology improves techniques of observation, measurement, and dissection. A great deal has been discovered, of course, but the root problem remains unsolved. No one knows how the initial impulse to action is generated in the brain.

For obvious reasons, my thoughts turned to this question as I found myself, much to my astonishment, getting out of bed. How was it possible that after all these years and all these man-hours of research, so little was known about the process that made such behavior possible? To my knowledge, I had not *decided* to get up. I had felt no *impulse* or *desire* to get up. Free at last of muscle cramps and restlessness, as well as the memories of activity that had evoked such sadness in contrast to my present situation, I had finally begun to grow comfortable with my immobility. Yet there I was, climbing out of bed and making my way toward the kitchen! Why? Had I been propelled in this direction by one particular group of cells or a complex, perhaps diffuse, shift in my neurochemical metabolism? If the movement came from a specific group of cells, were they located in the Motor Region or (as father claimed) in those highly convoluted areas, called the Frontal Lobes, which leave one, when destroyed by lobotomy, devoid of ambition, desire, and hope?

Of all the experiments I remembered, the one that seemed most relevant had been performed in the late 1970's at the University of Minnesota. A group of college students had been wired up to electroencephalograms and instructed to move their fingers whenever they felt an impulse to do so. The experimenters knew that such movement would be preceded, if only by a microsecond, by a discharge in the Motor Region. To their surprise, they found that the motor discharge was itself preceded by another, at a point near the midline between the Left and Right Hemispheres, some distance away from the Motor Region. In other words, a *causal impulse* had been isolated! A specific location within the brain had produced an *impulse to action*, which in turn had activated the Motor Regions, which in turn had activated the finger! Obviously, it was tempting to conclude that such an impulse had preceded my getting out of bed.

But pleased as I was by such a thought, I could not deny that it left me with the same question that had been raised in response to the experiments in Minnesota. Granted that an impulse to action had preceded the action itself, but what had preceded the impulse? Getting out of bed was more than a simple decision to move one's legs, arms, etc. A *plan of action* was involved, a *consideration of alternatives*. Granted something had moved me, but what was it? What was its source? *What caused the movement that moved me to move?* If we really mean to understand volition—why one moves his finger, for example, or why one gets out of bed—we have to locate, not just the cells that initiate activity, but *the cells that cause them to do so.*

Entering the kitchen, I leaned against the refrigerator and rubbed my eyes. Definite changes followed at once. Though I did not know where I was, the word "tea" was vividly projected, as if on a screen somewhere inside my brain. A visual rather than a verbal perception, the word had weight and physical dimension, even luminosity. Certainly it was more like TEA than "tea." In addition to this, it lifted my spirits immeasurably. As for its meaning, I can say for sure that it was "coffee."

I filled the kettle and put it on the fire, then took some coffee beans out of the freezer. The coffee-grinder made a whining noise that brought Marcia running from the meditation room.

"My God!" she cried. "You're up!"

"Of course I'm up," I said. "What's so strange about that?"

I put my arms around her and drew her close, kissing her on the forehead. "How about some tea?"

"Tea?"

"I was just making some."

"Since when do you put tea in the coffee-grinder?"

"Coffee-grinder? Yes, of course. How about some coffee, darling?"

"No thanks. I just had tea with Sonsei."

Gripping me by the shoulders, she leaned away from me in order to look in my eyes. "Thank God," she sighed. "I was really scared."

"Scared? Why?"

"I don't know. Maybe I'm not as brave as I thought."

"What's to be brave about?"

"Oh, come on, Drogin. Don't be dense. I thought you were sick. I thought you had brain damage."

"Brain damage! Ha! Ha! Don't be melodramatic, darling. I was working."

"Working! That's your idea of work?"

"Well, not exactly work, but—"

"What then?"

"I don't know. It's something I've wanted to do for a long time. For years you see patients with symptoms while you play it safe yourself. Holding back, hiding behind your authority, your clinical detachment. I always knew that if I really wanted to understand their symptoms I'd have to experience them myself."

I should say, I think, what must be obvious to the reader, that these words were not premeditated. I was moved to speak, it seemed to me, by the same sort of

forces that had got me out of bed. Mother claimed that
this was a form of "denial," a means by which I "escaped
responsibility," but in no way could I believe that what
I said was thought before I said it. Whether I agreed or
disagreed with the positions I took, it seemed to me
that each word was produced by the one that had
preceded it and that all of them were driven—like an
automobile by its engine—by Marcia's presence before
me. It was as if she'd triggered a neurological tape-loop
that I had neither the power nor the urge to alter,
interrupt, or (in this sense, mother was correct) own
up to.

"Do you mean to tell me," Martha continued, "that
you just sort of made up your mind to have symptoms?"

"Mind? No, mind had nothing to do with it. In the
beginning perhaps, I saw my opportunity and seized it.
But by the time I realized what I'd done, it was too
late to turn back. It was like an earthquake in my brain.
No memory, thoughts out of control, all my language
either incorrect or suspect. Christ, I couldn't even remember your name!"

"Were you afraid?"

"Afraid? Well, maybe I was. Yeah, of course I was.
But fear somehow encouraged me. Sort of like proof,
you know, that I'd made the right choice. If you want
to learn about your brain, I figured, you've got to take
some chances with it. Alter your relationship with it.
Stop deferring to it, you know what I mean? Stop thinking it will collapse or disintegrate if you challenge it or
question its authority. I know it sounds crazy, honey,

but everything was visible! I was tracking impulses
through my brain the way we track them on rats in
the lab. Impulse to get up . . . I saw it develop in the
Frontal Lobes! Impulse to speak, impulse not to speak,
impulse to laugh, impulse to drink tea . . . I saw them
all as if through some sort of incredibly powerful microscope. But what do you think this does to a brain,
to observe itself so closely? Everything turns inside out!
Because the impulse, instead of proceeding naturally to
its conclusion, activating motor cells, for example, so
as to move a particular muscle, is inhibited by another
impulse, the one that's observing its progression. And
the effect of this secondary impulse is interference, a
sort of neurological static that in the end produces the
opposite of what you intended. Call it perversity, call
it brain damage. The one thing I know for sure is that
the brain does not take kindly to this sort of self-
examination."

"I don't understand," Martha said.

"You don't?" I wasn't surprised at that. My words
had left me absolutely confused. "But it's obvious!" I
cried.

When the kettle whistled, another tape-loop began.
I made my coffee like an automaton. From the moment
I poured the grounds into the filter paper until all the
water had dripped through them, I was conscious of
nothing else. Facing the stove, I watched the pot with
riveted, almost maniacal fascination. Each drop, landing
on the surface, seemed a sort of miracle, and as the
familiar aroma reached my nose it produced an ex-

citement that was almost hallucinogenic. I had turned away from Marcia for what must have been nearly five minutes, and now, turning back with cup in hand, I was astonished to find her in front of me.

"Hi!" I said.

"Hi," she said.

"How are you?"

"Fine. How are you?"

"Very well, thank you. How are you?"

"Drogin."

"What?"

"Stop it, please. I beg you."

I took a sip of coffee and held it in my mouth for several seconds before I swallowed. I was thinking "coffee," but in vain. The name of the substance was "tea." Needless to say, I was desperate for caffeine, but my impatience in this direction made me apprehensive. I had not forgotten how the brain reacts to impatience, how often, when rushed, it responds with resistance, giving you precisely the opposite of what you want from it. How many times had coffee made me drowsy just when I needed most for it to wake me up?

I sat down at the kitchen table, and Marcia sat across from me. "All right, tell me!" she said. "What did you learn?"

"When?"

"This morning. From your so-called 'symptoms'."

I took another sip of coffee. "I don't know what you're talking about."

"Cut it out, Drogin. Don't fuck around. You just finished telling me—"

"Listen," I interrupted, "I'll say this once, but never again. When a man sets out to explore his brain, he's got to expect it to resist him. If he means to see it clearly, he can't expect for it to help him. It's no holiday, dammit! The first thing he has to relinquish is explanation. Clarity, continuity, conceptual description—all of it falls away! You do it all the way or you don't do it at all! What sort of trip do you take if you put one foot in the boat and keep the other on the pier? Goddammit, Marcia, it's the brain that makes explanation! It's the brain that connects one moment with another! How real can your symptoms be if it's clear to you why they're there?"

She leaned away from me and cocked her head. " 'Marcia'?" she said.

"What?"

"Did you call me 'Marcia'?"

"What?"

"You heard me."

"No, I didn't."

"Drogin: why did you call me 'Marcia'?"

"I called you 'Marcia'?"

"You know you did."

"Well, why should I not?"

"Well, for starters, darling, because 'Marcia' is not my name."

Feeling cornered, I tried my best to look her in the

eye and found myself, almost at once, looking at the ceiling. "Are you sure?"

She tried to smile, then changed her mind about it.

" 'Martha!' " I cried.

"No, Isaac. Not 'Martha' either."

"Come on, honey. Don't kid around, okay?"

"I'm not kidding. Are you?"

With no idea what I should say, I considered one answer after another, searching amongst them as one might among items at a supermarket. There was great tension for a moment. Each response seemed equally attractive. But when I made my choice, I felt relief and a sense of accomplishment.

"Of course I am!" I cried.

"Well, that's enough, okay? For one day, I think we've had enough, don't you?"

"You are my wife, aren't you?"

"Drogin! Stop it!"

I finished my coffee. As far as I could discern, it had not affected my neurochemistry. While one hand clung to the mug, the other opened and closed beside it.

"Don't tell me!" I said. "I've got to find it myself!" And then, after a pause: "I have it but I don't. Just when I'm about to remember it, I forget it again. I knew 'Marcia' was wrong. 'Martha' on the other hand seemed okay. How is it possible that what seems correct to one part of the brain can seem incorrect to another? What's the neurochemistry of 'seeming correct'? God, Marcia, I'm in love with my brain!"

"I told you: I'm not 'Marcia.' "

I slammed my fist on the table. "Goddammit, don't
you think I know that? Can't you take a joke? Don't
you think I know my own wife's name?"

"All right then, if you know what it is, why don't
you just sort of whisper it in my ear?"

Feeling defensive, I took a deep breath and leaned
back in my chair. As a result of the caffeine, my thoughts
were racing, and because of that I did not think to
blame them on caffeine. For that matter, I did not even
think that they were racing. In fact, it seemed to me—
since racing thoughts, by definition, prevent one's thinking clearly—that I was calm. "I've never felt such happiness," I said.

"You don't seem very happy to me."

"Well, maybe I'm not. To tell you the truth, I'm no
more sure of 'happiness' than I am of 'Marcia.' "

Marjorie placed her hand on mine. "Honey, do you
want to go to the hospital?"

"Hospital?" I touched my ear. "Do I hear you correctly? My ears must be deceiving me!"

I placed her hand on my cheek. The word for "fear"
was not available, but the feeling gripped me all the
same. "Don't abandon me!" I whispered. "The difference
between 'Millie' and 'Martha' is the difference between
courage and cowardice. If I don't push it all the way,
I might as well forget it."

"So!" she cried. "You knew it was 'Millie' all along!"

" 'Millie' is right? All this time it was 'Millie'?"

She shook her head in anger. "Oh God, please stop
it, Drogin. This is unbearable."

"Well, how do you think I feel?"

She stood up and backed away, staring at me with a bewildered expression, almost as if I'd punched her. So many times I'd seen these eyes—fear and sorrow, rage and disbelief—on those who were facing those with brain damage, but only an instant passed before she collapsed in a fit of laughter. There's the brain for you: frightened one moment, joyous the next. It wasn't a happy sight. Convulsed with sobs, chest heaving, face contorted like a clown's, she might have been having a seizure.

I found her grotesque but even so I joined in myself. My laughter began as a flutter in my throat, but within seconds it had invaded my body, wave upon wave erupting in spasms. My head bobbed, my stomach rose and fell, tears rolled down my cheeks, and I grunted as if in pain. I felt like a wind-up toy. If my brain had a role in this, it was not one of which it allowed me any knowledge. In fact, as far as I was concerned, both it and I had disappeared. For the next three or four minutes, I was nothing but this laughter. No memory, no expectation, no words and no desire for words, no thought, no fear, no questions, no answers, and of course no brain damage: how can there be dysfunction without function?

Toward the end it became extremely unpleasant. My stomach cramped, my throat burned, and my mouth was stretched and frozen in the direction of my ears. Breathless, sweating, we fell into each others' arms and slid to the floor as if in a faint. Reaching inside my underpants, Millie gripped my cock with a sweating hand. Until that minute, I had not been aware of my erection. It seemed a foreign object, like a tumor in my groin.

"Oh my darling!" she gasped. "Fantastic! Suddenly everything is clear! I don't know what it's all about, but every time I turn around you show me something new. Dammit, you're opening my mind! Pulling the rug out from under me! All these years I've been chasing after teachers when the only one I needed was right before my eyes!"

She unbuttoned her jeans with her free hand and pulled them and then her panties down to her knees, then climbed on top of me and guided my cock to the edge of her cunt. Her eyes ablaze with excitement and confusion, she was determined to finish what she had to say before sex made her forget it. "Please, my sweet, don't be afraid. Don't let anything hold you back! Whatever I say, whatever anyone says, you've got to take this all the way!"

CHAPTER EIGHT

During sex, all the voices fell away except the one I had mistaken for my own. Calm and reasoned, completely detached, it was very difficult, as I've said before, to believe that it originated in my brain. When people speak of their "innermost thoughts," it must be this sort of discharge they mean, cells that speak as if from the mountain top, describing the landscape below. Authoritative and sympathetic, but just a little patronizing, its tone was not unlike that with which I addressed my sicker patients in the hospital. Hard to say exactly where such a voice originated, but if I could guess, I'd place it in the region we call the "Reticular Formation" or the "Waking Brain." Located in the brain stem, which is to say just at the top of the spinal cord, the Waking Brain is generally thought to control attention and awareness—all the fluctuations, in effect, between "distraction" and "concentration." Rats with electrodes implanted there have been shown to learn mazes faster than those without. In humans, current theory has it that, while a great deal of information is always circulating in the cortex, none of it "registers" until it is received and processed in the Waking Brain. Isn't it reasonable to assume that voices of the sort that addressed me now would originate there as well? Where else would one find cells in which the discharges—consistent and orderly and most important, intimate, convincing—seem so different from the usual clamor emitted by the brain?

Like father's, the position taken by this voice was diagnostic, but it was more specific and persistent in its observations, determined to get to the bottom of my problem. While acknowledging that I was "clearly dysfunctional," it suggested that my principal symptom was self-doubt, the suspicion that I was malingering. "What we have to ask ourselves is whether there is a lesion, malfunction, or injury that will cause a man to discredit his own disease, accusing himself, even when it's at its worst, to have taken it on intentionally. Certainly, no tumor or anuerysm will cause such behavior. These are local phenomena, causing damage in one particular cluster of cells, which other cells can read without ambivalence. A tumor, for example, may cause a man to say 'blond' when he means 'brown' but not, adding insult to injury, to accuse himself of having done so on purpose."

After considering and discounting numerous alternatives, it concluded that the only reasonable explanation for my behavior was a diffuse epileptic syndrome that was causing random misfirings of neurons throughout my brain. Though I'd never heard of such a syndrome, I became convinced instantly that this was the diagnosis for which I'd been searching. What elegance in the notion of cells misfiring inexplicably! Such pathology could be the source of almost any symptom! Even if one were normal one moment and abnormal the next, commenting on his symptoms as if they were well under his control, epilepsy could explain it: it was consistent with inconsistent behavior; cells that misfired inexplicably would also misfire erratically; and such erratic discharges could easily produce periods of equanimity just after outbursts that had left one feeling deranged.

A sense of discovery welled in me, a belief that I was poised on the verge of a clinical breakthrough. Watching my symptoms, I grew more and more excited. So much so that, when the last shreds of reason and logic deserted me, I was excited by this as well. It was precisely because I did not trust what I was thinking, I thought, that I could believe in it. Precisely because my exhilaration was hysterical that I must embrace it. To be exhilarated in the midst of such a nightmare, to suspect that this exhilaration was the essence of the nightmare, what more could one ask who had committed himself to investigations of the sort in which I was engaged?

Finally, mind spinning, I shook my head in a kind of delirium, thinking: "Blah, blah, blah." And because these words meant absolutely nothing to me, they caught perfectly the happiness I felt, my absolute freedom from meaning or its absence, stability or chaos, hope or despair. How better than "Blah, blah, blah," I thought, to sum up the benevolence and compassion I felt toward myself, the spirit of adventure with regard to which my ever-increasing anxiety offered all the proof I needed that I was on the road to bliss? The word for "bliss" was "death."

Millie was ecstatic. She had never known such sex, she said. Her orgasm was an explosion, a volcanic eruption, a conflagration that extinguished her. Partly, she knew, she owed it to the laughter, but there was also the fact that I had opened her mind by destroying our "habit" and "familiarity." At first, she said, it had upset her when I had forgotten her name, but now that she'd got through this "superficial response," the blow to her pride, the "ego-deflation," etc., she saw what a "teaching" it was. Being stripped of one's name was no small thing, she said. How better to be reminded of the degree to which identity was delusion, the price one paid for the whole farce of personality?

"After all, what's the meaning of a name? What do we use it for? Isn't it just a label to which we become attached, a way in which we convince ourselves that what we are today is what we were yesterday? Just because I used to be 'Marcia,' do I have to be 'Marcia' now? Let it be 'Millie'! Let it be 'Marjorie'! Even better, let it change from moment to moment! Why should my name be constant when I myself am changing all the time?"

We were naked on the kitchen floor. Resting on her arm, facing the ceiling, my head was paralyzed, it seemed to me, by the weight of my brain within it. I had never been so aware of its size and density. While my ejaculation was in progress, it had been silent, no less reticent than during our fit of laughter, but now, with mother and father competing with my "innermost thoughts," it was more cacophonous than ever.

Despite the fact that I felt nothing that resembled what I recalled as sexual desire, my cock remained erect and throbbing. Lying on her side with one leg thrown across my thighs, Marcia stroked it gently while she whispered in my ear: "It's still hard. Do you want more? I feel like I could go on all day. I've never known anything like this! All our habit, it's fallen away. I thought we'd got too used to each other, but God, it's like we just met! I feel like you're a stranger! You don't know me and I don't know you! Did you feel it? Was I new? God, I love you! I've never been so happy!" She rolled over and sat on top of me and guided my cock into her again. "Am I too wet? Tell me who I am! What's my name? What's yours? No, of course you won't answer! You're playing for keeps, aren't you? You really don't know me! You never saw me before!"

Again my brain was silent while my cock was inside her. An odd experience, it was as if it—my brain, I mean—had relocated, taken up residence in my genitals, as if my head were between her legs, as if the warmth and wetness of her cunt surrounded my thoughts and sucked away every trace of memory or language. All of which made it more surprising that my articulations were appropriate. "Ah!" I cried, and "Oh, Jesus, yes!" and, as I ejaculated, "Oh! Oh! Oh!" as if in pain.

I believe I've said this before, but I hope I'll be forgiven for noting it once again: of all the lessons that brain damage offers, none is so poignant or valuable as that which concerns the brain's desire for functions it has lost. Even for those who detest memory, the need to remember grows stronger, not weaker, as the walls of amnesia thicken. Look at the first sentence of this paragraph. What does it prove except that, however much I yearn for incoherence, I cannot escape the need to describe such yearning coherently. Why should we be surprised that the instinct to survive is seen, not just in the species or in individuals, but in every organ of which individuals are composed? Amnesia and muteness are death to the brain, and like death they are resisted, even by brains for which the next stage of evolution is believed to be self-annihilation. How else to explain the fact that, with nothing to say and no urge to speak, no memory of speech, no capacity for speech, and certainly no sense of anything missing in silence, I turned to Millie and whispered in her ear: "Blah, blah, blah."

Please don't misunderstand me. This was not, like other incoherence, intentional. I had never uttered words of which I was more certain that the language regions of my brain had produced them independently and that regions dealing with plan, initiative and meaning were not involved.

"What?" said Millie.

"Blah, Marjorie! Blah, blah! Oh God, what death this is!"

Laughing aloud, she spoke as if to herself. "No compromise, right? You break with logic, you break with logic! It's as simple as that, right?" She kissed my ear and drove her tongue to a great depth within it. "Know what I feel? Anything is possible! All our habits have fallen away! No fear, no limits, no identity! We've obliterated everything!"

I studied the ceiling. Above the stove cracks in the plaster wandered across the surface the way my thoughts, as I saw it, were wandering through my brain. Idly observed at first, the cracks suddenly mobilized my concentration. Sitting bolt upright, I felt as if a light had gone on within me. All that had been dispersed was suddenly focussed and illuminated. Millie was "Millie" and I was "Drogin," and my "symptoms" were failures in judgment, taste, or understanding, matters of psychology perhaps, but certainly not neurology. I was convinced that my brain was normal, astonished and ashamed of myself for the way I'd been behaving. "Jesus Christ," I cried, "what the fuck is going on?"

"What?" Millie said.

"Please forgive me, Millie. Oh, Jesus. This has gone too far."

"What has?"

"This whole game. All these so-called 'symptoms'."

"Cut it out, Drogin. You can't be serious."

But I was. Shaking my head like one emerging from a trance, I had never been more serious in my life. "I don't know what came over me. What is this, some kind of theater? Psychodrama? Why on earth would anyone want to act as if he's brain damaged? Me of all people! Who knows better than I what brain damage really is? How can I play with it? How can I treat it like a game? It's inexcusable!"

Millie sat up. "Oh no, you mustn't say that! It's not a game! Don't reject it, darling. It's more than you imagine!"

"No," I said firmly. "I know how you feel, but believe me, it's totally perverse. Some sort of weird sadistic trip I'm on, torturing you as well as myself. It's as if I feel a compulsion to explore what frightens me the most. Like some people feel an urge to jump out of windows, I'm driven toward aphasia, amnesia, the whole gamut of neurological dysfunction, even epilepsy. Chaotic thought, incorrect language, God knows why, I seek them out, indulge them, cultivate them like a skill I'm trying to improve. Why else would anyone pretend to forget his own wife's name? It's as if I want to undermine my brain, distance myself from it, even treat it as an enemy."

Thrilled by these words and the conviction they generated, I stood up quickly, went to the bathroom and splashed my face with cold water. When I returned a moment later, I had so much energy that I was clapping my hands and crying "Yes! Yes! Yes!" in a strident, high-pitched voice that sounded nothing like my own. No way to contain such excitement, the joy I felt that the nightmare was over. Standing over Millie, I rotated my head, swung my arms from side to side, and bent from my waist to stretch the muscles in my back.

"Hey! How about some coffee?" I said. "How about some espresso?"

After filling the kettle without waiting for her reply, I continued exercising. So expansive was my mood that every thought seemed like insight, every insight revelation. Not only had I resumed my ordinary life, but I understood completely what had driven me away from it.

"Sure, it's intriguing," I explained, "to experiment with one's brain. One tries to disarm it, see what sort of quirks one can produce. We're all aware of the line between normal and abnormal function, so it's natural—especially if we're interested in neurology—that we become fascinated by what's on the other side. We want to see what's organic and what isn't, what we control and what we don't. You understand: what's determinology and what's philocology. Even now, as you see, the temptation remains—to sort of lean beyond my consciousness, speak without forethought, stretch my brain, explore the peripheries of language-function. And who knows? If you work at it with enough conviction, maybe you can succeed. Right now, for example, I've felt the temptation and I've made the effort, and to tell you the truth, I have no idea what I'm talking about. What, for example, do I mean by 'philocology'? Did I choose the word intentionally or did it happen without my knowledge? What's knowledge? What's intention? Those are the questions I mean to answer, darling! Philocology! Determinology! What could be more obvious?"

Slipping into her jeans, Millie's face was a mix of bemusement and effort, a yearning for concentration. "Say that again?"

"Well, the way I see it, there are two possibilities. On the one hand, certain brains may become too conscious of themselves. In order to function, a brain must forget itself. We all know that consciousness can interfere with behavior. Neurological behavior is particularly compromised by awareness of its source. While engaged in speech, for example, we cannot be conscious of the fact that speech derives from actual brain tissue without affecting that tissue and inhibiting its function.

"But it is precisely such knowledge that dominates my brain! It is tenaciously, relentlessly aware of itself! And of course what looks like brain damage to us may in fact be a result of such awareness. The real difference between my brain and other brains may be that mine is aware of the pathology that other brains take for granted.

"Now, why should this be so? A whole lot of work's been done on habituation and sensitization. It is well documented, for example, that even in simple organisms the nervous system becomes hypersensitive to positive stimuli that are repeatedly followed by those that are noxious. Once conditioned, they overreact in situations to which untrained organisms are indifferent. Who knows? Maybe my brain's just hypersensitive! Right now, for example, though it seems to be involved in an act of reasoning, it is actually focussed on the neurochemistry that makes such reasoning possible. And such self-awareness, impressive though it is, sets up an interference pattern that interrupts normal brain-function. The result—how can it be otherwise?—is confusion, disorientation. One speaks, as I am speaking now, with no understanding of what he's saying. Coherence, if it happens, is accidental. Every sentence stands apart from the one that precedes or succeeds it, and very often, by the time one completes a sentence, there is no memory of where it began. This is because the cells from which he derives his language are being observed by cells adjacent to them. Interference! Follow me? How can you think about something if you're thinking about thinking about it?"

Millie had buckled her belt, and now she was slipping into her shirt. "You said there were two possibilities. What's the other one?"

"The other? That I have established at last a realistic relationship with my brain. Most of the time, you see, when brains are functioning correctly, they generate belief in what we call 'the self' or 'the mind.' As I see it, certain cells assume authority with regard to the rest of the brain. They seem to be apart from the brain, independent of the influences to which other cells are vulnerable. When a man tells himself to concentrate, to 'make an effort' in one direction or another, it's these cells that are discharging. Somehow we've developed the notion that other cells obey them, and therefore, that by means of their initiative, our behavior can be controlled. This illusion—what we call 'self-control' or 'self-discipline'—is a function of the so-called 'normal' brain.

"For reasons we've never been able to understand, the belief in a 'self' or a 'mind' external to the brain has been selected during the course of evolution as advantageous to the species. Only in brain damage is it dissolved. When the symptoms begin to proliferate, when cortical behavior begins to break down, there's no way the belief in 'self' survives, no way you can pretend that you and your thoughts and your memories and all other aspects of what you call your 'self' are anything more than flesh. That's what brain damage teaches us! That's why I'm determined to investigate it! Once I understood that the belief in 'self' was the ultimate neurological function, I had no choice but to sabotage my brain by every means available."

I did not realize that the kettle was whistling until Martha moved to turn it off. Not the least disconcerted, she was smiling, it seemed to me, with affection, even devotion. "Shall I make the coffee?" she said.

I fell to my knees. "You've got to help me! I can't stand it anymore!"

Laughing, she shook her head. "Get up, darling. I get your point. You don't have to—"

"Get up?" Falling forward, I pounded my head on the floor. "For God's sake, Millie! Have mercy on me!"

She kneeled beside me, gripping my face in her hands. "What are you talking about? What's come over you? Are you serious?"

"Serious? I've never been more serious in my life!"

She lifted my face so that our eyes met. Inches away
from me, her devotion had given way to sternness,
defiance. "Don't give in!" she hissed. "Whatever you
do, you mustn't submit!"

"Submit? Give in? What are you talking about?"

"You know perfectly well what I'm talking about. If
you're gonna push it, you're gonna push it. There's no
such thing as a halfway solution. You made your move,
and now you've got to pay the price! Now you'll find
out what you're made of!"

I stared at her, astonished. Tears were streaming down
my cheeks, and every now and then a sob broke out,
but her response had quickened my thoughts and cleared
my mind. "What are you," I said, "wacko or something?
You're looking at a man with brain damage, and you
tell him to push it? Push what? Push with what? Who
pushes? What's pushed? Come on, Millie! Aren't you a
nurse? Don't you recognize disease when you see it?"

"No! No!" Her eyes were shining. "You're just scared!
You're out on a limb and now you're afraid the limb
is gonna break. And who can blame you? No, don't
think for a minute that I blame you! You've risked
everything! You've got more courage than anyone I
know! You've challenged your brain! Rebelled against
the tyranny of thought! The whole charade of language
and memory! Only now your brain is fighting back!
That's what's happening! Don't you see? *Your brain is
fighting back!*"

Though shocked at first by what she said, I found
myself, to my surprise, agreeing with her, convinced

that I must point myself in the direction she suggested. Then I realized that I could not remember that direction, could not in fact remember anything she'd said. It was while searching my memory for her advice that I struck her—very hard, with my open hand—and sent her sprawling on the floor. "Blah, blah, blah!" I cried.

She sat up quickly. Her face was flushed with anger and confusion but her voice was very calm. "Be careful, Isaac. You know I can hurt you. Don't push this too far."

"That's better," I said.

" 'Better'?"

"Yes, 'better.' "

"What do you mean by that?"

"I can't say. The word is unclear."

"Oh Jesus," she sighed. "You're one persistent son-ofabitch, aren't you?"

"No, I don't think so." I stood up and put the kettle on the stove again. "It's not persistence. If you want my honest opinion, I think I'm just playing. The idea, I think, is to treat the brain as a kind of toy. If you can approach it like that, with a light heart and a sense of humor, its power is dissolved. Yes, there's the truth of it, Millie! A man who can play with his brain can play with anything! Nothing can hurt him, nothing can frighten him, nothing gets him confused. He's faced the worst that life can offer and treated it as a game!"

Still on her knees, Millie's eyes were closed, her hands cupped in her lap, her lips softened and curled into a beatific smile. "I can't say I understand you, but then again, the step you've taken is by definition beyond understanding. All I can say is, I'll be here when you need me. I swear it, darling. Whatever you ask, if it's within my power, it will be done."

"Are you sure?"

"Yes. I'm sure."

"Promise?"

"Yes, I promise."

I took her in my arms. "This afternoon, I might have seizures. Grand mal or petit mal, I can't say yet which it will be. Maybe it has to be both. Promise me you won't panic, all right? There's no way I can do what I have to do if I'm not willing to have seizures. No matter how difficult it gets, no matter how sick I seem to be, give me your word that you'll stick by me and wait it out, okay?"

"If I've stuck it out this long, why should I back down now?"

"Are you afraid?"

"Of course I am. So what?"

"You mustn't believe a word I say, you know."

"How about you? Do you believe it?"

I ignored her question. "Speaking incorrectly, that's the main thing. Say what you don't mean, betray your thoughts, put one over on your brain. When symptoms aren't available, invent them. Have you ever heard such nonsense in your life?"

"No," said Millie, smiling happily. "I guess I never have."

CHAPTER NINE

The snow had stopped, and a bright winter sun had broken through the clouds. Suspended in the glare, objects were lucid but oppressive to the eye. The more I wanted to see, the more my eyes resisted. Squinting and blinking as I looked around, nothing but light seemed to register in my brain. Objects emerged from the light, then disappeared within it. Memories remained of what I'd seen, but I couldn't easily distinguish them from other memories, visual memories evoked by the effect of light on my brain as a whole.

The literature is vast on optical stimulation. There's no shortage of documentation concerning light's influence on regions far removed from the Optic Lobe. I saw the ocean, for example. Morning light glistening off the stream where father and I were fishing for trout. I was not so dysfunctional that I believed such images real, but on the other hand, when the hospital loomed in front of me, I could not completely reject the thought that I might be hallucinating. Fearful, but angry at myself for being afraid, I turned to father and mother for help, but what I got was argument that, if anything, distracted me all the more.

"What's this about trout?" father said. "I never took him fishing."

"That's a lie," mother said. "You know as well as I do . . . every summer from the time he was nine . . . Vermont, Maine, New Hampshire. Don't do this, Maxwell. Memories like this are just what he needs to restore his confidence. He's played with his brain enough. It's time he got serious. He doesn't need you to confuse him now."

"Don't tell me about memory. Who knows memory better than I do? The holographic theory, the protein theory, the Corpus Callosum, the hippocampus. You worry about yo-yos, I'll worry about memory! It's you who's confusing him, Alice, not me."

"Alice" and "Maxwell" were not their names, but neither complained about being misidentified. Without agreeing with or listening to each other, they went on like that for several minutes while I stood looking at the hospital. Twenty-five stories high, its white brick facade was vibrating, slipping in and out of its background so that often it seemed like empty space. Its color at its base was indistinct from the snow, but its windows flashed like strobes in the sunlight. The whole effect was raucous, festive; it lifted my spirits immeasurably.

That I did not know how or why I'd come to be there seemed a stroke of good fortune. It was true, I had to admit, that I recognized the building, even remembered that I worked there, but these were long-term memories; I'd never meant to see them disrupted. If anything, it was essential that they be maintained so that my loss of short-term memory could be appreciated. A man who lacked both short-and long-term memory would never undertake the experiments in which I was engaged. No trauma, however great, would compromise his equanimity. Unable to remember what he was meant to be, he'd barely notice what he'd failed to be, and without that comparison, he'd lose all interest in exploring what he was.

Pushing through the revolving doors, I paused to examine the lobby. Imagine my disappointment when a succession of names appeared! "Wall," I thought. "Lamp. Guard. Elevator. Table. Carpet. Floor." This sort of compulsive naming, an attempt by the brain to reassert its authority, is common among the brain-damaged. I've had patients who spent the better part of their waking time testing their memory and language, seeking information (old telephone numbers, for example, metric equivalents, the age at death of past presidents) that normal brains would never retain, and accusing themselves, upon failing to produce it, of symptoms far worse than those from which they actually suffered. One would have thought I could avoid this problem, but to my surprise I was not only enthusiastic about the names I produced, but also applauded myself when the word I wanted and the word I found seemed more or less identical. This quickly does the brain outflank us! Those objects—the rubber tree in the corner, for example, the

guard's hat—that proved unnamable left me feeling no
less bereft than they would have before my illness. Was
this a sign that my conviction was imperfect? Was it
possible that behind my excitement with dysfunction
there lurked a secret desire to resume, vis-à-vis my
brain, the relationship I'd once considered normal?

Testing myself, I tried naming things incorrectly. The
lamp became "the hat," the floor "the ceiling," the
carpet "the hospital." Of course I got nowhere. I had
forgotten that labels involve the participation of many
regions of the brain, not only those that produce a word,
for example, but also those that produce belief in its
veracity. What good does it do to call the floor "the
ceiling" if somewhere deep in one's brain a voice cries
"floor! floor!" with such confidence and authority that
"ceiling" crumbles in the face of it? One could as easily
stop a tank with his bare hands as challenge the brain
with this sort of exercise.

Despair gripped me until I saw my mistake. Once
again, I hadn't gone far enough. Belief was the symptom,
not language. The very fact that "floor" was backed
with absolute conviction was proof that it was incorrect!
And similarly, the pleasure I'd taken in "correct" language was all the proof I needed that it was anything
but so. The man before me was no more "the guard"
than he was "the lamp," and whatever else it might
be, the object on the floor was not "the carpet." Why
should I trust my brain to verify my language? Was its
opinion of words any less diseased than the words
themselves? Let it cry "floor" all day and all night!

Once I knew that "floor" was the symptom, "ceiling" assumed an authority equal to that of "guard" and "elevator," but with this difference: nothing in my brain celebrated it, nothing endorsed it as correct. And of all the strategies I'd attempted, none, I thought, had been so elegant as this, so swift in its effect on my condition. It was one thing to name an object incorrectly, quite another to maintain the error after it was recognized as such. The first was mere resistance, superficial rebellion, but the second challenged the brain at its source. By denying it the right to decide between true and false, I had rendered its greatest weapon obsolete.

The guard was a large black man, perched on the edge of a high metal stool. He was drinking coffee from a styrofoam container, smoking a cigarette, and reading a newspaper spread out before him on the counter of the information booth. To my amazement, he greeted me as if we were acquainted. "Hi, Doc. Working on Sunday?"

I studied him closely, unable to place his face. "Hello, Edward," I said.

"Operating or just looking in on patients?"

"Operating."

"On Sunday? Emergency?"

"No, just looking in on patients."

"God bless you, Doc."

I stood almost at attention, as if waiting to be dismissed. Though still convinced I did not know him, I had to admit that "Edward" had rung the very bell that "Marcia" had before. It seemed a remarkable piece

of neurology that one could know the name of a man
one had never seen before. But then again, wasn't the
converse also true? Hadn't my brain often tortured me
with faces I knew but could not name? "And God bless
you," I said.

"Thanks, my man."

Leaning forward, I placed my palms on Edward's
newspaper and spoke to him confidentially. "If I could
understand the project, I'd get on with it. No fear, you
understand? I don't mind confusion, but just for starters
I'd like to know what I'm trying to accomplish. I don't
think that's too much to ask, do you?"

"Lord, no, man. Everyone got the right—"

"Then again, a man who trusts his brain for questions
has got to trust it for the answers too."

"Exactly!"

"Exactly?" I stared at him with a disbelief that I
myself did not believe. So quick and complete was my
change of mind, however, that between my new point
of view and the one it had replaced I saw no contradiction whatsoever. "What do you mean 'exactly'? Are
you out of your mind? A man cannot exist who doesn't
trust his brain! Can you imagine what it means to be
suspicious of your thoughts? To think to yourself, 'This
thought is a symptom'? To call a man 'Edward' and
speak to him as if he is your friend when you never
saw him in your life? To call that—" I pointed at the
floor—" 'the floor' even when you know it is 'the ceiling,'
and to tell yourself, even when you see your mistake,

that you called it 'the floor' on purpose? I tell you, Maxwell, you don't know what freedom is until you've challenged your brain like this! This is joy, my friend! Nothing holds me back!"

Edward squinted and cocked his head to the left. He had moist, sorrowful eyes and a bush-like Afro that made his hat look bouyant on his head. "Tell you what, Doc. You give me some of what you're on, I'll give you some of what I'm on. Then we'll have our conversation."

I closed my eyes and pondered what to say. Given the *cul de sac* into which I'd driven myself—logic abhorred and memory abandoned, thought received as neurochemistry—it was not an easy decision. A man who rejects his brain can say anything he wants, but how is he to choose among his options? I decided to say the first thing that came to me, speak as it were "off the top of my head," but to my surprise, my mind was a blank! It was almost as if the search for thought had made thought disappear. Cluttered and frantic just moments before, my brain was stripped, a womb-like, empty space in which no movement could be discerned. For an instant I thought it silenced forever, but even as my excitement mounted, I saw that I'd misread it once again. In my hunger for thought, I'd failed to notice that I'd been thinking all along!

"There are ten thousand million neurons in the human brain," I said. "They're connected by a thousand times that many synapses. Are you laughing at me?"

"Fuck no, man. Why should I do that?"

"What is it then? Brain damage or freedom from my brain?"

"Beats me." Edward closed his newspaper, then carefully folded it in quarters and placed it beneath his elbow. "Tell you the truth, Doc, I think you got me confused with somebody else. You talkin' to someone you ain't talkin' to."

A silence ensued. I was trying to figure whether the foregoing conversation had been coherent or incoherent, and whichever the case, if I had intended it to be so. Was it correct to have said 'Are you laughing at me'? If not, had I said it against my better judgment or because of it, because my "better judgment" had insufficient influence with the language regions of my brain or because it had been alert, once again, to the dangers of language and coherence? In short, who was in charge, and why? For the most part, I continued to feel that my mouth and voice were apart from me, that what I said was not being processed in my consciousness. This alone should have told me that, coherent or not, the conversation had not proceeded according to my intention, but the matter was complicated by the fact that separation of speech and intention was what I'd wanted all along. How could I be disappointed that I was not behaving as expected when expectation, of all neurological functions, was the one I was most determined to sabotage? It didn't matter what I said as long as I did not intend to say it!

With a burst of affection, convinced somehow that I owed these insights to him, I extended my hand to Edward. "Go fuck yourself," I said.

He got down from his stool and leaned across the counter of the information booth. "Say what?"

A woman who looked like my mother propelled her wheelchair toward the doors that led to the street. Watching her turn so that she could open the door with the back of her chair, I was suddenly aware, for the first time, of other people in the lobby. Two children and an elderly man sat on a couch in the corner, and my father, wearing dark glasses and a leather jacket, paced to and fro in front of the elevators. I thought: I've made a mistake, taken the wrong direction. The thought that I am sicker than I thought cannot be celebrated without its being undermined.

"You heard me!" I cried, backing away from the information booth. "Get the fuck out of my way!"

"Use your wrist," father said. "Lay in the fly so that it raises no water where it lands. There's a place in your brain for the trout, and a place in the trout's brain for you. Once you connect them, your hook will find its mouth unfailingly."

Walking backward, my eyes fixed on Edward, I bumped into a chair, then a table, then another chair. A standing metal ashtray hit the floor with a crashing sound that echoed through the lobby. Each collision increased my excitement. I felt unleashed, free of all restraint, completely convinced of the choices I'd made, and as before, endless gratitude toward Edward, a belief that I owed all this to him. Running for the elevator, I cried, "I'm sicker than I thought! Do you hear me? I'm sicker than I thought!"

Edward jumped the information booth and ran after me, reaching the elevator in time to hold the door with his hand. "Hey, Doc, wait up!"

Music was playing on the speakers in the elevator. Feeling cornered, I pressed my back against the wall of the elevator until I heard it. "What's that song?" I cried.

Edward looked up, fixing his eyes on elevator speakers as if he could see the music. "Wait a minute," he said. "Ain't that 'Oh Susannah!'?"

" 'Oh Susannah!'? Yes! That's it! 'Oh Susannah!'!" I sang,

> Oh Susannah!
> Don't you cry for me.
> I come from Alabama
> with a banjo on my knee!

Edward nodded when I was done. "Yeah," he said. "That's it all right."

"Did I get the words?"

"Seem like you did. 'Course, 'Oh Susannah!' ain't exactly in my top ten, but—"

"But where did they come from? Tell me that, Maxwell! A man who doesn't know the difference between the floor and the ceiling produces lyrics he hasn't heard in twenty years!"

"Shit," Edward laughed. "That ain't nothing. I got the Supremes, all of Otis, Aretha, B. B. King, Stevie Wonder. They be in my head sometimes when I don't even want them there. All morning I been listenin' to

Sam Cooke! You think I want Sam Cooke? I can't stand the motherfucker!"

"But it's a miracle! Don't you see that? Sam Cooke is a miracle! 'Oh Susannah!' is a miracle!"

"Miracle? Maybe Otis a miracle, Doc, but Sam Cooke? I don't see no miracle there."

"Oh Susannah!" was gone and "Silent Night" had replaced it. Gazing up at the speakers again, Edward closed his eyes with a soulful expression. When he looked at me again, his face was sad and protective, almost maternal. "All right, Doc, now tell me the truth. Tell me what the trouble is."

Elation welled in me. The nightmare continued, but for an instant I knew it to be one from which I had awakened. A deep crevice had opened, something beneath the neurology with which I was acquainted, and I spoke fast because, as I saw it, I had to catch the words before my brain could take them away. "I don't know," I said.

CHAPTER TEN

As the doors of the elevator closed, vibrations rippled my right forearm, wrist, and fingers, and left in their wake a tingling sensation, as if my arm had fallen asleep. Familiar though I was with psychomotor epilepsy, I took these symptoms, not as the first indications of seizure-activity, but as a sign that my brain, in response to the three magical words I'd spoken to Edward—"I don't know"—had gone into a spasm. Why? Because if there's anything the brain can't tolerate, it's *acceptance of incapacity.* As long as it can generate desire—for memory, information, happiness, explanation, correct neurological function, truth, etc.—and the disappointment it produces, it remains in a state of relative equilibrium. It's no exaggeration to say that neurological health is at its optimum when desire is at its height. But let it diminish, let one say, in response to inaccessible memory, "I don't know," or in response to unhappiness, "I don't care," let one adopt, in relation to his symptoms, a light-hearted, or even better, a hopeless attitude, and spasms of the sort I felt cannot be avoided. This was why I interpreted these first signs of epilepsy as a sort of temper

tantrum on the part of my brain, and even now, aware
though I am that the explanation itself may have been
a product of my seizure, I cannot reject it unequivocally.

As the elevator rose, I kept my eyes fixed on the
indicator above the door. It was a bank of lights in the
shape of arrows on a chrome-plated band that spanned
the width of the doors. From floor to floor, the lights
progressed from left to right, illuminating "1," then "2,"
then "3," etc. Since "2," for example, went on at the
very instant that "1" went off, the indicator usually
appeared to be a single light in motion rather than a
series of lights in sequence, but for me, with my internal
clock almost at a stop, its progress seemed completely
discontinuous, separate lights going on and off with long
intervals and no illusion of movement between them.
Between "1" and "2" nearly five minutes seemed to
elapse, and by the time the indicator reached "3" I felt
I'd been in the elevator for something like half an hour.
I had no memory of my conversation with Edward,
none of saying, "I don't know," and despite the fact
that my arm remained numb below my elbow, no memory of my seizure.

When the doors opened at the tenth floor, I got off
without knowing why. This was the operating floor.
The nurses' station stood opposite the elevator, the
locker rooms at the north end of the hall, and at the
south, a pair of swinging doors that led to the operating
rooms themselves. Even on Sunday, there were patients
lined up on stretchers in the hall. Nurses, interns, and
residents, all of them dressed in the pale green shirts

and trousers we used as operating garb, moved back
and forth among them. On each of the stretchers the
patient's chart hung on a clipboard, and most had IV
bottles suspended above them. Two of the patients were
neurosurgical. Even though I couldn't see their faces, I
knew them by their newly shaven heads.

Mother and father were speaking at the same time
in very low whispers that I could not understand. Now
and then I made out a word—"hippocampus" or "malingering," for example—but nothing more. Occasionally,
my "innermost" voice could be heard as well, but that
too was indecipherable. I was feeling slightly dizzy but
also excited, so I believed the dizziness to be a happy,
lightheaded sensation. As before, my confidence verged
on bravado.

When I opened the door to the locker room, I found
Eli sitting on the couch. He was barefoot, legs folded
beneath him, drinking coffee and eating a chocolate
donut. Two shy, the box of six from which he'd taken
the donut was on the couch beside him. A workaholic,
he was the only one on our staff who regularly operated
on Sunday. He was still wearing his operating greens,
his shirt and pants streaked with blood. He spoke with
a mouthful of donut. "I just did Phyllis Chandler. You
were right about her, boss. That's the biggest fucking
tumor I've ever seen. I'd be surprised if we got 30
percent of it."

The locker room was softly lit, carpeted in thick
brown pile, its walls covered with textured fabric that
matched the rug. There was a small refrigerator in the

corner, a coffee machine, a television set mounted on the wall and, on a black formica desk, a white telephone for outside calls and a beige one that connected to the central dictation equipment on which we recorded our notes after surgery. Loudspeakers on the ceiling broadcast the same recorded music that played throughout the hospital. I poured myself a coffee and sat down in the leather easy chair that faced the couch. Father sneezed.

"God bless you," I said.

"What's that?" Eli said.

"Look here, Elmore. Everything's okay. Let's get that straight before anything else. Whatever I do, whatever I say, don't worry about me. There's nothing wrong with me, nothing going on that I can't handle."

With a shaking hand (his tremor generally returned within a quarter hour after he left the operating room), Eli picked up the box of donuts and offered it to me. " 'Elmore'?" he said.

"No thanks," I said, taking one from the box.

"You called me 'Elmore.' "

"No, I didn't."

"You know you did. C'mon, Izzy. What's going on?"

I shrugged my shoulders. My arm was trembling again, but it seemed to me I'd willed it to do so, activating my nervous system by means of concentration. In fact, like the dizziness I'd felt a moment before, the tremor seemed a pleasant sensation, not unlike the first effects of alcohol. Convinced that I'd finally achieved the control of my brain that I'd been seeking all along,

I felt pride and excitement, an astonishing sense of power. When the room began to change a moment later—the rug going from brown to orange, the overhead lights becoming so bright they hurt my eyes—I found the changes perfectly reasonable, a kind of exercise I'd undertaken as a test of my authority. In fact, it seemed to me that the whole of my perceptual system, like a staff of loyal servants, awaited my commands.

"What's going on?" I said. "I'll tell you what's going on. Every once in a while a man is given a chance to see the Truth. Through some combination of luck and circumstance to break through the ideas he normally takes for granted. I need your help. I beg you not to listen to anything I say."

Eli's back straightened. "Say that again?"

I leaned forward and spoke in a whisper, as if afraid of being overheard. "Here's the thing . . . you know we've both been interested in brain damage for years. Why? Because normal brains are facades, obstacles. Because the better they function the more they enslave us. But sometimes you have to leave the realm of speculation and take a leap into reality! It's not enough just to be interested in brain damage. You have to experience it directly! Embrace contradiction! Forget memory! That's what I've done, and I don't regret it! You've got to believe me! I don't regret it! No matter how much I bitch and moan, don't be misled. I wouldn't have it any other way. You think a damaged brain is less than a normal one? No, Elmore, it's the normal brain that's really damaged. Having a brain—that's the

real brain damage. What we call brain damage . . .
that's freedom! Revolution! How can you find what's
behind the brain if you can't take a stand against it?"

Suddenly exhausted, I took a large bite of the donut
and, turning it with my tongue, let it sit in my mouth
unchewed. It wasn't long before it changed like the
carpet had. Its taste went from sweet to bitter, and its
texture became brittle, almost crunchy. Again, there
was no doubt that I had accomplished these changes
on my own. I thought: a man who can initiate a tremor
in his arm or change the color of a rug can easily control
the receptor cells on his tongue that produce the experience of taste. Once again, the familiar sense of pride
and accomplishment welled up in me.

"Well, I give up," I said. "I don't know what the fuck
I'm doing anymore."

Eli laughed. "And seeing as how such knowledge is
a product of the brain, I guess I should offer my con-
gratulations."

I went to the coffee machine and refilled my cup.
The donut was finished, but the taste—acidic now, like
vinegar—remained in my mouth. Further inspired by
this achievement, I decided to shift my priorities, work
on my olfactory perception, producing random odors on
command. Shit was my first choice, and like the carpet,
it presented no problem. No sooner had I sought the
stench than it was overwhelming! The room stunk so
badly that I felt on the verge of vomiting!

"C'mon, don't be an asshole, Eli. Can't you see I need
your help?"

"Yeah? And what sort of help would that be?"

"Well, that's obvious, isn't it? If someone came into my office talking like this, I'd sure as hell have a look at him."

"But I'm the police! Since when do revolutionaries ask the police for help?" He stood and went to the sink in the corner and threw some water on his face. "Look here, boss. I'm glad you're enjoying yourself, but to tell you the truth, I don't find this very funny. I know you love the game you're playing, and if it weren't me you were playing against maybe I'd enjoy it too."

"Playing? Who's playing?"

Smiling broadly, I leaned forward and vomited on the rug. The odor of feces had got the best of me, of course, but not for an instant was I discouraged. If a man could control his visual and olfactory functions, I reasoned, why not his autonomic nervous system? Perspiration, breathing, the whole of his digestive system—why should anything be beyond him? And how better to demonstrate his powers than by forcing his stomach into spasm, constricting his breath, producing cold sweat on his forehead, and finally, this rush of heat, these contractions in his throat, this wretched gagging as he regurgitated and spewed the contents of his stomach onto the floor?

Faced with such evidence, how could I doubt the choices I had made? This was the jackpot! The beginning of the end! What more could I ask of my investigations than the chaos and fear that I felt now? To feel at once an absolute terror and a faith in that terror's meaning and beauty was to play this game at its highest stakes, with all risks, including the possibility that it was not a game at all, pushed to the brink of tolerance. Heaving again, I understood not only that the worst and best were yet to come but that, by depriving myself of distinctions between them, I had a chance to make them identical. There's nothing I won't do to make this happen, I thought, even if it means backing down.

Eli hurried to the bathroom and returned a moment later with a damp towel. "Jesus," he murmured, wiping my face. "You really are sick, aren't you?"

Slipping an arm around me, he helped me out of the chair and guided me to the couch. He unzipped my jacket and pulled it off, slipped a pillow under my head, loosened my belt, took off my shoes and covered me with a blanket he got from the closet. Finally, bringing water from the bathroom, he lifted my head and held the cup to my lips. "Okay, Izzy, give me some chronology. When did all this begin?"

The water soothed my throat and made me realize how sore and parched it had become. Even as I spoke, I felt like a coward, a hypocrite, a man who'd seen the Truth and turned his back on it. I couldn't believe the words coming out of my mouth.

"I don't know," I sighed. "It came out of nowhere. Everything turned upside-down. All of a sudden, everything was discontinuous, interrupted. Memories dissolved, words lost all connection with their meanings, every thought was contradicted, nothing endured for more than an instant. But worst of all was the way I embraced it. You heard me—sabotaging my thoughts, laughing at my fear of it, playing with my confusion as if it were a game. What I couldn't forget, I pretended I'd invented. I've never known such chaos. As if part of my brain was driving me to undermine the rest."

By the time I'd concluded this little speech, I was believing what I said. Far from feeling like a coward, I was beginning to think I'd come to my senses. That's how the brain works. If a few cells turn in one direction with a certain amount of enthusiasm, many more are sure to follow. A smile unfolded on my lips. No mockery here, nothing capricious or perverse. Drinking from the cup he held to my mouth, I had simply agreed to be his patient.

"Whew! Thank God that's behind me! It's over now! Suddenly I feel completely calm. No, more than calm. Cleansed somehow. As if waking from a nightmare! Whew! That was close, wasn't it? It happened so fast! Before I knew it . . . boom! Know what I mean? Of course you do! Yes, completely calm! Jesus, how can I thank you? God knows where I'd be without you!"

Eli lowered my head and crumpled the empty cup in his hand. "Izzy?"

"Yes?"

"Have you been having trouble with your eyes?"

"No."

"Headaches?"

"No."

"Weakness in your arms or legs?"

"No, why do you ask?"

"You know why I ask."

He went to his locker and searched the pockets of his ward coat, returning a moment later with his opthalmascope. Aiming the light into my eyes, he checked the size and shape of my pupils, their response to light, their consensual reaction, and finally, bringing the light between them, their convergence. Leaning so close that our foreheads nearly touched, he shined the scope into each of my eyes in turn and directed me as I had directed so many patients myself. "Cover your right eye and focus on my left. Now my right. Now cover your right eye and look into my left. Now my right. That's good." He raised his hands and spread his fingers. "Tell me when you see a finger move."

When finally he paused to write in his notebook, I said: "You know you won't find anything in the Occipital Lobe."

"Right. And from the way you're talking and understanding me, I'd say there's nothing in the Temporal Lobe either. No lesions anyhow. Of course, we can't really say until we've checked you out completely. Do you feel well enough to come up to my office?"

I shifted on the couch. It seemed to me that something had struck me in the middle of the back, but I considered the feeling "imaginary." Besides, more pressing things were on my mind. The sense of myself as a patient had had its own effect upon my brain. Eli's attentions were not only comforting me but arousing yearnings for diagnosis and explanation, a belief—a hope!—that before very long my symptoms would be cured. Maybe I'm brain damaged, I thought, but at least I don't want to be.

"Why are you laughing?" he said.

"Because you're so naive. For all your experience, all the patients you've seen, all the symptoms you've diagnosed, you're as gullible as a first-year medical student. How could you let me take you in? Don't you know the difference between brain damage and malingering?"

Why did I say this? Because to my astonishment, the yearning for brain damage was thriving on the fact that I had turned against it. It was one thing to conclude that the desire to sabotage one's brain was symptomatic, another to reject such desire because of this conclusion. For me, it seemed, quite the reverse was happening. What was wanted most was wanted least. Dread and desire were nourishing each other. Just when I thought I'd arrived at my "innermost" conviction, I'd come upon a deeper conviction that demanded betrayal of the first. To feel a wish was to create longing for its opposite, and no desires could be sustained but those for which no thoughts could be found to support them. Now I knew why epilepsy had appealed to me. Because nothing horrified me more. And this realization, far from quelling my desire, intensified it. No more tremors, it was full-scale seizures I wanted, fear in its ultimate amplification, adventure of the sort that one could never comprehend. The need for help was nothing beside the desire for helplessness, and the longing for calm and order was dwarfed by the joy I felt in the screams that even now were collecting in my throat.

The seizure began with a repetition of its precursors. The rug turned orange, the lights glared, tremors rippled my arm and fingers, and finally the odor of shit surrounded me. Also repeated, just before the first convulsion, was the earlier hallucination that had granted me views of my brain's interior. I saw not only the cells in which my seizure originated, but those others, the ones I hated most, which made it seem a cause for celebration. When the screams broke free, they were less shrill than I'd expected, more like animal grunts than shrieks of pain or terror, but the convulsions were exactly as I'd hoped and feared, violence beyond thought, dazzling displays of sound and light, surges of force as if from electrical shock, my body leaping on the couch as if every cell had become autonomous. My chest heaved, my arms and legs flailed in all directions, saliva foamed on my lips, and my hips lunged and recoiled as if on springs.

Thoughts were very clear. I knew that I had seen beyond my brain and that my brain would never permit me to remember what I saw. Finally, pausing briefly on the edge of consciousness, I remarked as if for the first time that my view of all this was external, that I was watching myself from a point directly overhead. The body gyrating on the couch was not my own. I felt the seizure's power, but empathetically, as if it were happening to a friend I loved but could not help, and

I heard my screams like a recording of someone else's voice.

I awoke to find myself on the floor with Eli beside me, holding a tongue-depressor in my mouth. Sweating, shivering, eyes out of focus, it took me time to find my voice, but when I did, my meaning was clear, my pride unmistakable. "Well!" I said. "What do you think of that?"

"What I think doesn't matter," he said. "All I know is what I see. This afternoon we'll get you a CAT scan and an EEG, and then, hopefully, we'll get to the bottom of this."

CHAPTER ELEVEN

Wearing a small backpack, her meditation cushion under one arm and a sleeping bag under the other, Millie arrived early that evening with the intention of staying as long as I was in the hospital. She was radiant, effervescent, years younger, it seemed, than the person I'd seen a few hours before. Her eyes burned with conviction, shifting between fear and excitement, focussed one moment then suddenly restless, skittish, darting about like a fugitive's. I thought she looked a little crazy, but with my language no less skittish than her eyes (the hat she placed on the bed, for example, was an "umbrella"), I was hardly in the mood to credit such description. Why trust "crazy" when you can't find "hat"?

As far as I could see, she was in no way disconcerted by the circumstances in which we found ourselves. She explained that a few hours ago, at the dojo, she'd experienced "a breakthrough" in karate, an "opening" that came as close to "Deep Enlightenment" as anything she'd ever known. While sparring with a man whose skills had always been superior to hers, the space between them had suddenly dissolved.

"There was no separation between us!" she explained. "No difference between him and me! It was as if I knew in advance what he meant to do! When he kicked or punched, his hands and feet came at me in slow motion. All these years he's handled me, but today I handled him as if he were a White Belt!"

The backpack contained her toothbrush, a book on Zen and another on Sufism, a nightgown, a portable coffee pot, a small bag of freshly ground coffee, and all the items she required for setting up her altar. After placing her meditation cushion on the floor in the corner, she set her Buddha on the window sill, her incense holder in front of it, and a tiny water bowl in front of the incense holder. With my approval, she lit incense and made us coffee. Only then, when she'd brought the coffee and settled into the chair beside the bed, did she acknowledge our surroundings.

"So? What's going on?"

"Who knows?" I said.

"You do, that's for sure."

"Me? Ha! I know nothing!"

"Of course not. That's just the point, isn't it? As you said before, why put one foot in the boat if you keep the other on shore?"

"I said that?"

"You don't remember? No, of course not. You have to forget it, don't you? That's what it means to leave the shore behind! How can you live in the present if you're clinging to the past?"

She was wearing a yellow turtleneck sweater and gold loop earrings, rings on three of the five fingers on her left hand, two of five on her right. Her short hair covered her ears and fell in bangs across her forehead. Freshly washed, blacker somehow than before, it seemed youthful, the hair of a seven- or eight-year-old girl, and I found my eyes returning to it whenever I lacked a word ("window" and "books" at present, "hat" still, and very briefly, a moment before, "hair") or suspected I'd misused one. For reasons I still don't understand, something about her hair seemed to render such concerns irrelevant; as if, when I looked at it, the sections of my brain that produced my anxiety were either less insistent or broadcasting on a frequency to which I wasn't tuned.

With a conspiratorial air, she said, "I know you don't want me talking about it."

"Talking? About what?"

"You know what I mean."

"No, I don't."

She smiled knowingly, but then her face became severe, almost stern. "Sensei saw what was happening. When sparring was over, he called me into his office. He said I was fighting like a master. Last week I'm a first-degree Black Belt, today a third or maybe even a fourth. What's going on? 'It's Drogin!' he says. 'What else can explain this sudden change in energy?' I knew he was right. How could I doubt it? I said before that you've taught me something, but I didn't realize how deep it went, how much you've undermined my ego. I know you don't like this sort of talk, but what is it except ego that keeps us separated from other people? That's what karate is all about, you know. If you want to defeat your opponent, you've got to love him, and in order to love him, you've got to give up the ego that separates you from him. It's not you and him, it's you and you. When you are him and he is you, that's when there's love, that's when the fight is over. But that sort of thinking, it's death to the ego. And what is the ego but brain? That's what you taught me! What we call 'ego' is produced by identification with the brain. We think we're our brains, therefore we think we're our egos. And once we think we're our egos, we think we're this tiny self separate from other people. 'Me' and 'you,' 'this' and 'that'—where except in the brain—in memory! in language!—do such concepts originate?

"What you've made me see is that it's my brain that keeps me separated from my opponent, my brain that controls the speed of his foot as it approaches me. It's my brain that ruins my energy, my brain that creates my ego! The brain creates anger and violence, hatred and conflict. The brain creates war! That's what you've taught me, darling. Religion, meditation, the martial arts—they're nothing but . . . neurology! Just different techniques for mastering our brains! I know I shouldn't speak of such things, but I can't help myself! You've opened my eyes! Brought me face to face with brain damage! I want the world to see what I see now! Teachings like this—they don't belong to any one person. They have to be shared! There's no one alive who wouldn't benefit from what you've taught me today."

A silence followed during which she gazed at me with increasing devotion. I don't know if I returned her glance because at that point I felt another seizure coming on. Like the one I'd had with Eli, this one too seemed a course of action on which I had embarked with forethought. That is to say, while she was talking, I had *decided* to have another seizure, and now, as I felt the decision taking effect, it wasn't fear I felt but *annoyance with myself* for having made a foolish decision. Such was my condition, you see, that no condition in which I found myself could seem entirely unpremeditated. I know now of course that this disruption of the decision-making process was an effect rather than a cause of epilepsy (grandiose visions of self-control being a common sign of seizure-activity in the brain), but still, it seemed to me, when the seizure began, that I was nothing more or less than a man who'd got what he desired.

Most of what I went through now—the optical and olfactory hallucinations, the convulsions, the screams and grunts, the exquisite microscopic view of my brain as the seizure overwhelmed it, etc.—was familiar. When I awoke, I felt the same pride, the same excitement, and not surprisingly, Millie seemed to share this feeling with me. If what she'd seen had bothered her, she certainly didn't show it. When finally I was calm again and sitting up in bed, she gripped my hand and said that nothing she'd ever witnessed had moved her so deeply. I'd seen people go crazy from watching seizures, but never with such enthusiasm. She said she'd never seen such energy. Who could deny that all the gates were open, all the energy in the universe passing through my mind?

"I know some people would be afraid of seizures, but how can I be intimidated when you prepared me for them yourself? The way I see it, seizures are nothing more than your brain's resistance to the energy you've released, a violent attempt to keep you under control. They ought to be celebrated as a a sign of liberation rather than treated as disease!"

As I say, the effect of epilepsy on the brains of those who witness it cannot be underestimated. What made it worse, in Marjorie's case, was that she was echoing what I took to be my own irrationality, the absurd romanticism with which I had surrounded my symptoms and which now I seemed unable to control. "That's beautiful," I said. "Thank you, darling. You can't imagine what it means to know you understand."

Tears welled in her eyes. "I'm only keeping my promise," she said. "Considering how much you've given me, that's the least I can do for you." She leaned and kissed me, first on the forehead, then on my eyes, finally on the lips. "Your courage is awesome!" she whispered. "You don't back down from anything!"

I listened to my reply with astonishment. "How can I? This is my work! My duty!"

"My God, yes. And what a work it is. What a duty

you've taken on for yourself." She looked away from me and took another sip of coffee that must have been lukewarm by now. "Funny thing," she said. "I can really understand why people are afraid of seizures. I don't deny I felt a sort of terror myself. But what is terror? Doesn't it originate in the same brain that produces seizures? The way I see it, all fear is egoism. The ego establishes itself in a certain equilibrium and then it fears anything that threatens it. But what's equilibrium? Memory, right? The brain remembers where it was a moment ago and wants to remain in the same place. Suppose one didn't have such memories or, even if his brain produced them, he didn't get attached to them? What would happen to the fear? How can you fear to lose something if you never got attached to it? And what makes you get attached except your brain? That's how I see it, darling! Once you see the brain for what it is, how can anything it does disturb you?"

Closing her eyes and taking a deep breath, she suddenly gripped my head as Sensei had. Her lips trembled, and I thought I saw her nodding slightly as she pressed her fingers into my scalp. "Yes," she said, releasing her grip, "Sensei was right. He said that now I'd be able to feel the energy myself. Jesus, darling, there's tremendous power around your head! It's like a magnetic field!"

"Sensei," I said, "is an idiot."

Her eyes flashed anger, but only for an instant. Once she'd processed my words and translated them into her private language, she saw them in a different light. "Of course. Who else but you would make that connection?

Sensei's genius lies in what he doesn't know, not what he does. Who knows that better than you? On our terms, being a genius and being an idiot are virtually the same!"

"The same? What do you mean, 'the same'? Give me that hat!"

"What hat?"

"The hat, the umbrella. Don't confuse me, Marcia. It's time to be serious."

Marjorie laughed. "Do you want more coffee?" She went to the altar and lit another stick of incense, then stood for a moment, looking out the window. I saw the reflection of her face in the glass and, on her mirrored face as well as her real one, the flickering headlights from the automobiles on the road beside the hospital. Naturally, they had given me the best room on the ward. From here, on the ninth floor, you could see the river and the smokestacks on the other side, bridges to the north and south draped with lights like holiday decorations. "The truth about the brain," she said, "is that it's time-bound. Isn't that the essential quality of all material things? It's always in the past or future, never in the present. It deals with concepts, ideas, memory, but it can't deal with immediacy, this very moment. It can remember this moment after it's happened, anticipate it before it happens, but it can't comprehend it directly. That's what you're after, isn't it? This very moment! The here and now! I keep forgetting that you'll never allow me to be content with anything I remember."

Since it's taken for granted in hospitals that doctors do not wait for patients to say, "Come in," Elmore knocked on the door and pushed it open at the same time. "Anybody home?" he said.

" 'Here and now,' " I said, "are words you've misused because of your aphasia."

"Thank you," Millie said.

"Hi, boss."

"Hello, Elmore. You remember Marcia, don't you?"

"Marcia?" Elmore smiled uncomfortably and leaned to kiss her on the forehead. "Hello, Marjorie."

" 'Marjorie'?" she said laughing. "Sorry, Elmore you've got it wrong. These days, it's 'Marcia.' "

"Yeah, I know what you mean. Not too long ago I was 'Eli.' "

He took half-a-dozen Polaroid prints from the breast pocket of his ward coat. "It's just as you predicted," he said. "The scan is completely normal."

I looked at the prints, examining them carefully for signs of a tumor or a bleed. Whatever was wrong with me, it had not affected my ability to read x-rays or, for that matter, appreciate them. There is nothing like a CAT scan for revealing variations in tissue density, or the size and shape of ventricles.

"What about the EEG?" I said.

"That's a different matter," he said. "We've got significant spikes in the left Temporal Lobe."

"Well, what do you expect?" I said. "You don't get grand mal seizures from athlete's foot."

Hands shaking, Eli searched his pockets and found a

pack of butterscotch Lifesavers. The paper rattled as he unwrapped first the outside package and then the individual candy. "No thanks," I said, when he offered me one.

"What do you think we should do?" I said.

"I don't know. We could wait it out, see if you stabilize, maybe do an angiogram tomorrow."

"No thanks, baby. I had another seizure just before you came. That's four in less than seven hours. Who knows what sort of damage this is doing to my brain? No, the one thing we aren't gonna do is wait. I don't want to fuck up anything that isn't fucked up already."

Eli's eyes were very uneasy. Had I been any other patient, he'd have looked at me directly, almost with affection, but now he stared at a point on the bed frame just above my head. Lights from the cars below flashed on the wall behind him. In the distance, I heard television sounds, different programs from rooms down the hall that either cancelled each other out or broke apart to allow an instant of singularity: an anchorman on the evening news, a beer commercial, gunshots. Behind them all, a constant drone, I heard the music from the speaker system in the hall.

Elmore said, "I think we could contain the seizures with Dilantin. Maybe a bit of phenobarb."

"No. No medication. Not yet anyhow. I'd like to play this out with a full deck. What's that you're eating?"

"Lifesavers. Butterscotch."

"Can I have one?"

"I just offered you one."

"You did?"

"Come on, you know I did."

Millie laughed. "Around here," she said to Eli, "what you did in the past is not what you did in the present."

"Beg pardon?" Eli said.

He offered me the candy again. "No thanks," I said.

He and Millie stared at me, but unlike her, he wasn't smiling.

"Nope," I said, "Dilantin is not for me. And God knows, not barbiturates. What I want most is to keep my head clear."

"What then?" Eli said.

"Why not go in and have a look? Would it scare you to do a craniotomy on your boss?"

"Well, it's a little soon to be thinking of that, isn't it?"

"Why?" I said. "You can't ignore my seizures, and you can't ignore the EEG. You know as well as I do that I'm an ideal candidate for surgery."

"Sure, Izzy, but Jesus—"

"I don't like it," Millie said. "I know I shouldn't butt in, but it seems to me you're seeking a medical solution for what is basically a spiritual problem."

"What do you mean, 'spiritual'?" Eli said.

"Don't pay any attention to her," I said. "We'll do her when we get done with me."

Reluctant though he was, Eli knew as well as I did that, when a patient who is seizure-prone refuses medication, you either let him go on with his seizures or, if it's surgically accessible, seek out the epileptic focus.

There was nothing unusual about me as a patient except my relationship to my surgeon and my knowledge of surgery, and it was precisely for this reason that the procedure intrigued him.

He fixed his eyes on me. He was silent, but his brain wasn't. I could see it processing the various arguments for and against what I had proposed. He knew the risks that we'd be taking, of course, but he also knew that this was an opportunity—to operate on a patient who could truly observe and report on his own brain during the course of stimulation—that would never be offered to him again. When a faint smile took shape on his lips, I wasn't the least surprised. There was no way, in a neurosurgeon's brain, that the few cells against this sort of research would win out over the legions that were behind it.

"Very funny," Marcia said.

"What is?" I said.

CHAPTER TWELVE

Is there a neurosurgeon alive who hasn't imagined operating on himself? How his brain might respond to seeing itself as mine saw itself that morning? Certainly, for surgeons like Eli and me, who operated on conscious patients, the dream of putting oneself on the table was almost irresistible. In fact, we had discussed it so often that the simple arrangements to make it possible had been clear to us for years. One cannot accomplish a craniotomy alone, of course, but by means of two mirrors—one clamped to the instrument stand above the table, another to a tripod that positioned it at Eli's left shoulder—I was able to observe it, assist in it, and most important, explore the effects of such observation and participation on the brain in which they occurred. If all neurology is ultimately circular, an attempt by the brain to understand itself, how could we have designed a more elegant experiment?

Angled to face each other, the mirrors provided me with a view that approximated the one I had when operating. Positioned in the sitting posture—which we preferred for surgery in this region of the brain—I saw the flap drawn on my newly shaven, anesthetized head, saw four layers of scalp and tissue peeled away, saw four holes drilled and connected with the power-saw, saw a rectangular section of skull removed, and finally, by means of the tiny scissors with which I had so many times performed this function myself, saw the final membrane clipped and drawn back to reveal my brain to me—and me to it—directly. The watery grey flesh that made it possible to see this watery grey flesh in the mirror. The convolutions marking the language area in which the word "convolutions" had been produced. The arteries that fueled and oxygenated the flesh and the blood vessels that drained it. The cells that produced the words "No, no, no," and those that produced the fear that I had made a terrible mistake, and those that produced excitement near to ecstasy, and those that produced the violent impulse, passing so quickly that it barely registered, to take hold of this flesh and tear it to shreds and end forever the noise with which it continued to bombard me.

Seeking to simplify the procedure, we used one of the older operating rooms at the north end of the hall. Its equipment was spare (no video or microscope, for example) but it was intimate and relatively private, and it offered us a chance to keep our staff to a minimum. For all the tension it could generate, seizure surgery was not overwhelmingly complicated. Since it was done under local anesthetic, you didn't really need an anesthetist, and with so few instruments required you could manage with very little nursing assistance. Since

Millie had worked in neurosurgical operating rooms, we had all the help we needed, as it were, in the family. I would never have risked such a set-up with anyone but myself on the table, but my first priority was to maintain the privacy of the room. I was not in the mood to explain or defend myself, and I couldn't think of anyone on my staff who would understand what I was doing.

The first view of itself caused certain changes in my brain that ought to be noted. It stood to reason that, without the firing of certain groups of cells in the flap that Eli had opened, what I saw would not exist for me. In other words, the image in the mirror both originated and terminated in itself. What I had assumed just a moment before to be the object of my attention I now knew to be its source, while "I myself," what before I'd taken to be the viewer, was actually the object. You may think that, caught between these alternatives, my brain leapt back and forth between them, but in fact it seemed to remain in suspension between them. Indeed, unless I'm mistaken, it entered now a period of relative inactivity. As I stared into the mirror (watching Eli cleaning the flap now, sponging the blood and cauterizing the few vessels that had not coagulated on their own), all "mental" activity came to a halt. The cells that produced what I generally took to be my consciousness ceased to discharge for a certain (to me, needless to say, immeasurable) length of time. There was no thought, no memory, no passage of time, no registration of the image at which I gazed, and none, of course, of the image at which it gazed. It was almost as if, by means of this direct confrontation, I had achieved the neurological silence which, a moment before, I'd thought to achieve with force.

My head rested on a black leather cushion, and a system of clamps secured it. A green sheet, almost the same color as the shirt and trousers Eli and Millie wore, covered my body. Though we had dispensed with some of the safety procedures we used with other patients, we had two IV lines installed—one in my right forearm for glucose solution and a drug that controlled my blood and intracranial pressure, another in my right thigh, to be used for blood transfusion if it should be required. Attached to my chest were electrocardiographic leads, and an oscilloscope mounted on the wall provided steady readouts of my pulse and blood pressure. Finally, small plates on my head provided a constant electroencephalograph that would track my brain waves and, we hoped, alert us to any sign of seizure activity.

I saw my brain within the flap like a picture in a frame. Its surface rose and fell with my pulse. The bone around it was approximately three-eighths of an inch thick, and the mid-cerebral artery, dark and thick as an earthworm, bisected the flap on a diagonal. In contrast to this artery, which looked to be drawn by a fat piece of charcoal, the lines formed by the blood vessels and the cortical convolutions were thin as gossamer, spreading like a spider's web across the surface of the flap. When the craniotomy was complete, the edges of the flap shaped to Eli's satisfaction with the small bone-clipping instrument we called a "rongeur," he covered my head with a towel and placed a hand on my shoulder. "How am I doing?"

"Perfect," I said. "I never saw a better flap."

"You okay?"

"Couldn't be better! What about you?"

"A little shaky, but I'll be okay. If you don't mind, I'll take a break for coffee before we begin the mapping."

As soon as he was gone, Millie came around the instrument table and took hold of my hand. A green paper mask covered her face, but leaning forward, she placed the paper on my lips and made a kissing sound. Above the mask, her eyes were shining, flashing almost, and her voice was breathless with excitement. When she spoke, the mask rose and fell like a tiny bubble as air moved in and out of her mouth. "Can I look?"

"Be my guest," I said.

She disappeared behind me and a moment later, in the mirror, I saw her hands remove the towel. It occurred to me that if my brain had really been looking at me before, it ought to be able to see her now. But I was wrong of course in my assessment of things: my brain was blind without my eyes. For some reason this struck me as an extraordinary revelation.

"Oh my God," she whispered.

"What is it?"

"I can't believe that it's really what it is."

"Maybe that's because it isn't."

She covered the flap again and came around beside me. I could tell from the lines at the corners of her eyes that she was smiling behind the mask. "You're the bravest man I know," she said. "One in a million, one in a million years."

Anger rose in me. "Listen, Marcia, or whatever the hell your name is, this is not a game anymore. There's one too many circles. I'm losing it, you understand? What I am, where is it? I'll never come back from this. I'll never be the same!"

"Exactly!" she cried. "Why should you? If you wanted to be what you used to be, you wouldn't be where you are. Listen, darling—you've got too much courage to talk like that. You've come too far to turn back now."

"Courage?" My left hand reached and took her by the throat and squeezed until she gasped. For a moment I thought it would strangle her, but then it relaxed its grip and fell back on the table. I felt tremendous affection for her.

"Isn't this great?" I said.

"God, yes," she said. "Even better than I thought. The teachings never stop."

For all the ways we'd simplified our logistics, the mapping procedure remained the same. It was quite routine for us now, even with me as the patient. Once the flap was ready, Eli wheeled the generator into place and connected it to the stimulator. Bracing his hand on the small armature we used for this purpose, he gripped the electrode like a pencil and held it almost parallel to the surface of my brain, bringing it in at a very low angle so as to set it down instead of aiming it. Viewed in the mirror, the black tip of the electrode looked like a sort of insect that had landed on the cortical surface. There wasn't much danger of penetration because the flesh at this point was so resilient (you could actually probe it with a finger without causing any damage), but it was very important to keep the tip on the surface so as to minimize the number of cells you activated. As before, stimulations were marked with numbered tickets of different colors—white for motor response, blue for language, orange for the miscellaneous "psychic" responses that occurred in the lower quadrant of the flap. The tickets themselves, like the log in which my responses were recorded, were Millie's responsibility.

As usual, we began in the Motor Region, a narrow strip of tissue that paralleled a long convolution—the so-called "Fissure of Rolando"—in the middle of the flap. When he activated the generator, the foot switch made a snapping sound. Under the sheet, my right thumb contracted, bending toward my hand as it did when I made a fist. When he released the switch, I heard the same sound, and then my thumb relaxed.

"Well?" he said. "Where are we?"

"Right thumb," I said. "Contraction."

Using a locking forceps, Millie removed a white label from a small glass container on the instrument table and passed it down, forceps and all, to Eli, who placed it at the point he'd just stimulated. It was oval-shaped, a glossy white plastic. In the mirror, it stood out like a shirt button against the oyster-grey of my cortex. The number "1" was clearly marked on it. Eli said, "White

ticket number one. Right thumb. Contraction," and then
Millie, transcribing his words like a secretary, entered
them on the chart.

That's how mapping went. For a moment I felt like
a surgeon again—the brain in the mirror might have
been someone else's. All the fear was gone, all the
excitement, certainly all the confusion. What I saw in
the mirror was a piece of flesh. Something you'd find
in a butcher's case. Only by an act of memory and
conscious choice would I think to call it "my brain."
When I flexed my thumb several times to prove that I
could do it on my own, it did not occur to me to ask
myself how I'd managed, "by myself," to activate—out
of the ten billion cells in my brain—exactly those that
the electrode had.

Ever since I'd begun to perform this kind of operation,
I had suspected that its true depths were not being
plumbed. The only way to do that would be to experience it first-hand. Only a few steps into the mapping
procedure I knew that such experience, and the data
it would produce, would exceed my wildest dreams. As
early as white ticket #4 I began to realize that the
simple responses that usually appeared on our charts—
"right thumb contraction," for example, or in this case,
a "pins-and-needles" sensation in the index finger—
were not the only ones the electrode produced. In fact,
they were but the simplest and most visible of a whole
spectrum of responses that involved many different regions of the brain. Here at #4, for example, stimulation
had indeed elicited, just as we noted on the chart, a

"pins-and-needles sensation in the index finger," but it had also produced both the now-familiar microscopic view of the cells that had caused this to happen and a heated controversy with regard to the validity or pathology of that vision. Father reminded me that it was almost a duplicate of those I had experienced during seizures, calling it "an hallucination," the result of "epileptic" firings in the Optic Lobe, but mother took issue with him. "Ask yourself, Herman, what is vision? What makes it possible? What do we mean by 'visibility' except the amount of light the eyes can receive and how the Optic Lobe processes it? Maybe he's seeing better! Maybe he's seeing things as they really are! Maybe it's you and I, with so-called 'normal' brains, whose vision is really distorted!"

I couldn't resist her argument. After all, the brain that had created the hallucination was also the one that sought now—with father's voice—to invalidate it. In fact, it was quite likely that the cells that had produced the word "hallucination" were not too far from those secreting the vision to which it referred. And while many parts of my brain continued to side with father, those that were most vociferous agreed with mother. As far as they were concerned, I had *actually* seen the activated cells transmitting their impulses to the cells adjacent to them.

Consider then, what I'd learned already about our charts. With any other patient, white ticket #4 would have had but a single entry: "Pins-and-needles sensation . . . index finger." In my case, however, if we wanted to be accurate, #4 should have had subheadings—#4.1, #4.2, etc. How else could we include the vision of the cells that had produced the sensation? Were we to deny that, like the sensation in my finger, it had been caused by the electrode? And what of that combination of auditory and language cells which, in the wake of my vision, had produced father's and mother's voices? What of the discharges that had produced words like "hallucination" or "epileptic" or "pathological"? And what of those cells in my brain which, in the face of such invective, remained convinced that what I had seen was true? Labelled correctly this stimulation, should have had at least five entries:

1. Motor function: pins-and-needles sensation, index finger
2. Optical function: view of discharging cells
3. Language/auditory function: father's voice; rejection of #2
4. Language/auditory function: mother's voice; endorsement of #2
5. Cognitive function: acceptance of #4; validation of #2

You can imagine my excitement when these ideas began to crystalize. More than at any time since I'd come into the operating room, I felt like a scientist again. To combine the present level of my optical function with the new charting procedure I'd just discovered—it seemed to me that with these tools I had a chance to understand the brain as it had never permitted itself to be understood before.

At white ticket #5, mother elaborated on her argument. What was happening, as she saw it, was that my whole perceptual apparatus had been liberated by the unique situation Eli and I had designed. Every cell in my brain—not just those in my Optic Lobe, but those that produced my consciousness—was firing with heightened efficiency. With time slowing down, I could pick up and chart neurological events that in the past had been invisible to me. I could see what I'd never seen, hear what I'd never heard, pick up stages in my thought-process that before had mingled and blurred into speedy continuums. It was as if I were watching a movie with a projector that permitted each frame to be studied independently. As if each cell in my brain could see itself as clearly as I saw the mirror above me or the sheet that covered my body.

"This so-called 'microscopic' vision," mother cried, "this so-called 'hallucination'—what is it but a view of reality? Isn't this what the brain is supposed to see? If things can be seen under a microscope, why not with the 'naked eye'? If a movie can show behavior in 'slow motion,' why not the brain? Doesn't it stand to reason that the brain should be at least as perceptive as the machines it has constructed? The 'naked' eye—why should it determine what's visible and what's invisible? Who can say what's 'normal' perception, Maxwell? Who can say which brain is 'damaged' and which is not? If his brain is released from its pathology, what right have we or anyone else to call it 'epileptic'? "

As Eli observed, my Motor Region, what we called the "Motor Strip," was almost classical. Every function was exactly where the textbooks said it should be. As the tickets accumulated, forming a jagged line down the middle of the flap, my brain took on the appearance of a medical illustration. Ticket #1, which had caused the thumb-contraction, was almost at the center of this string, with many labels above and below it. Moving down from it, the index finger was next to the thumb, the middle next to the index, the ring next to the middle, etc. Tickets #6 through #11 produced tremors, tingling or jerking movements in my right wrist, elbow, and shoulder; #13 through #18, the trunk, hip, knee, ankle and toes. Number 16 was a sharp twinge, almost a pain, in my right hip, #20 an itching sensation on the underside of my right testicle. Moving up from ticket #1, sensations were above my shoulders. Number 20 was in the neck, #21 the forehead, #22 through #25 the eyelid and eyeball, the last causing a dilation of the pupil that distorted my vision and caused both the mirror and the flap within it to dissolve into a blur. All other motor responses were facial. Number 26 produced a tremor in my right cheek; #28 through #30 vibrations, itching, and other sensations in my lips; #31 what Eli called, for the purposes of the chart, "an ironic smile," #32 and #33 tickling and tingling sensations on the tongue; #35 swallowing, #37 a "gulp" in the throat; and finally, #39 and #40, grinding of the teeth.

All fairly predictable as I say, almost academic, but there were several exceptions which, at least from my point of view, made the procedure unusual and at certain moments frightening. For one thing, as the cells were activated, I continued to see them at greater and greater magnifications, and for another, every response was charted in my mind with a compulsiveness I could not control. No entry had fewer than half-a-dozen subheadings and some of the subheadings had subheadings themselves. Under #22, for example, there was #22.1-#22.8; and under #22.2 there was #22.2-a, 22.2-b, and 22.2-c.

More disconcerting than any of this, however, the self-destructive impulse that I had felt at the first sight of my brain had reappeared at #8 (I had charted it as #8.3) and again, with growing intensity, at #10, #11, #14, #16, and every point thereafter. When speaking of this sort of operation, Eli and I had often speculated that the brain's response to viewing itself might be volatile, that it might even have some sort of auto-immune response to witnessing what it was not conditioned to witness, rejecting this view of itself as the body might reject an organ transplant. It seemed to me that this was happening now. Traumatized, my brain was turning on itself.

At first I tried to divest the impulse of emotional and psychological content. In its early stages, it seemed merely a discharge, a firing of motor neurons that drew my hand upward and backward, but only incidentally in the direction of my brain. This was white ticket #8.

When Eli deactivated the electrode and the impulse disappeared, I felt confident that my assessment had been confirmed. It was a strictly somatic response that involved no part of my body except my hand. But when it reappeared, at #10, it occupied not just my hand but the whole of my right arm. Furthermore, even though the somatic effect of the stimulator seemed to be limited to my right wrist and elbow, its underlying effect, as I came quickly to understand, was an agitation, an energy, a thrusting gesture that pointed, not just upward and backward, but—indisputably—in the direction of my brain. And while this gesture remained primitive and "physical" until ticket #14—an urge toward my brain but not yet an urge to destroy it—it began to change after that, growing more complex, as if being translated into emotional and psychological language, until finally, at #19, it was unmistakably destructive, exactly the urge I'd felt when my brain had first been revealed to me. It was as if every cell had mobilized behind this one all-enveloping desire—the yearning to be free of it, the brain's yearning to be free of itself.

Needless to say, the impulse was difficult to chart. Since many firings in the brain are often responses to responses that precede them, the initial discharge was always followed by others, as other parts of my brain became involved. Father and mother had their opinions of course, but in this instance, I had my own. At #19.2, for example, the impulse frightened me; while at #20.3 I welcomed it. There were two points (#20.4 and #22.3) at which I was certain it was "pathological"; several

(#23.5, #26.4, and #28.4) at which I believed it "imaginary"; and one (#21.4) at which I took it to be a joke.

Then too there were neurological interpretations. Sometimes (#25.1, for example) I hearkened back to my belief that it was a simple motor impulse; sometimes (#25.4) I believed it to originate in the mid-brain, the so-called "limbic" area, which produces more primitive emotional behavior; and once (#30.3-b) I saw it as a combination of motor and optic function, "an attraction," or a "desire for unity" between the neurons in my hand and the neurons in my optic lobe that made my hand visible in the mirror.

Nor should I forget the points (most clearly, #21.3 and #21.4, but also all the subheadings under #26.1) at which the impulse reversed itself. At these moments I not only felt no desire to destroy my brain . . . I felt the opposite! Far from destructive, I felt reverent and protective toward it, determined to see it cured, and thrilled at the prospect of using it again. The thought that I had once wished to destroy it was not only inexplicable but also,—taking me back to #20.4 and #22.3—"pathological." There was no way I could understand such an impulse except as an epileptic firing.

So far, of course, I haven't mentioned the larger implications of the impulse, namely its relation to the so-called "death instinct" or the "will to survive." Only toward the end of the Motor Strip, when I knew we were approaching speech tissue, did these issues arise, but when they did, they shed an interesting new light on the impulse I'd been tracking. The real question was:

if this were in fact a desire to kill myself, which cells, which region of my brain, had secreted it? In all the years I'd been performing this type of surgery, no patient had ever indicated that stimulation in the Motor Strip could trigger such wide-ranging effects on other regions of the brain. How could these circuits, long thought to be among the simplest and most linear in the cortex, be connected to cells that generated violent emotion, positive as well as negative? How was it that self-protection and self-destruction vacillated with place-ment of the electrode? Was it possible that the cells that generated the death instinct and those that gen-erated the will to survive were not only proximal but connected to motor tissue?

The forty-first stimulation, less than a millimeter an-terior to the one that had caused me to grind my teeth, elicited a sort of gargling sound, as if I were growling or clearing my throat. Since the demarcation between motor and language tissue is always unclear, we couldn't know for sure whether this was a motor response—one produced by cells activating muscles in the throat—or the first sign that we had crossed the border into the speech area. When the next three stimulations caused more specific vocal response—a dog-like barking sound, then a sort of whine, then the word "Yes!"—it was obvious that we had moved outside the Motor Strip. Martha closed the container of white tickets and opened the one that contained the blue. What might have been white tickets #41, #42, and #43 became blue tickets #1, #2, and #3.

Before proceeding, Eli fetched a Polaroid camera from the instrument case. At this point, we always photographed the flap to record the placement of the tickets and the distribution of motor cells. I couldn't see him behind me of course, but I heard him setting up the tripod, moving the camera close to the flap, and finally, snapping the shutter.

"Need a break?" he said.

"It's up to you," I said.

"I could do with some water. What about you, Martha?"

"Yes," Martha said. "That would be really nice."

I was feeling a bit uncomfortable, my back and shoulders and especially my neck stiffened by too much time in the same position. Either that or the stimulations themselves, which had caused so many discharges in the cells that controlled these muscles, had left a tension in their wake.

"Can I look?" Millie said.

"Why not?" Eli said. He was pouring water from a thermos we kept in the instrument case. Using a plastic straw that bent so as to fit behind his mask, he drank two cups. Then he poured two more and brought one to each of us.

Finding her gazing into the flap, he said, "Remember your neuroanatomy?" He took out the small penlight we used as a pointer and gave her a quick review. "This is the mid-cerebral artery, and this is the Fissure of Rolando. Forward from here is where the Frontal Lobes begin and back here is the Optic Lobe and the

Auditory. Where the blue tickets begin, of course, that's
the language region. It should go down to about here.
Below this fissure, what's called the 'Fissure of Sylvius'
we should begin to see psychic response. This area is
called the Interpretive Cortex. As a rule, it's not special-
ized tissue, like the motor or language region. The cells
have not been assigned a specific task—they're sort of
up for grabs. With stimulations down here, you never
know what you'll get. Emotional response, maybe memories, maybe hallucinations. Right about here, if our
predictions are right, we'll start to see some epileptic
discharge on the EEG."

A long silence ensued. I had the uncanny sensation
that I could feel Millie's eyes as she studied the flap.
Finally she sighed and repeated what she'd said before.
"It's hard to believe it's what it is."

"Is it?" Eli said.

"You don't feel that way?"

"No," he said. "To tell you the truth, I can't believe
it's anything else."

Blue ticket #4 was a soundless grimace, but #5 made
me groan as if in pain. That speech tissue connected
with tissue far removed from it I saw now by the fact
that the operating room was bathed in a halo of golden
light. Martha's face, the instrument stand, the mirror
and the flap within it—everything was luminous, radiant, as if direct sunlight on a midsummer day were
shining in the room.

At the same moment, my mood turned bilious. Though
lacking an object, anger rose within me until it seemed

to exude from my pores. Both the anger and the sunlight disappeared with deactivation of the electrode, but with the next stimulation, blue ticket #5, which made me laugh aloud, they reappeared in slightly different form. Now the light was closer to orange than gold, and the anger more like disappointment. Sadness loomed but did not seize me. Among my thoughts, a feeling of certainty appeared which, like my anger, had no particular cause, and then, once more, the microscope resumed. Flashing slowly, methodically, the neurochemistry of these impulses (feelings of certainty, visions of luminosity, anger, disappointment, etc.) appeared in vivid detail. The objects I saw seemed to be enlarged, as if the microscope had been raised to a higher power. As if I could see things now on a protoplasmic level. As if the neurons were no longer discrete particles but complex structures composed of smaller ones.

In effect I saw things the way we saw them under our newer, more powerful microscopes, when we studied biopsies in the lab. Each neuron seemed huge and complex, its various components clearly distinct from each other. I saw the nucleus and the cytoplasm and, near the cell wall, chains of chromosomes floating like underwater plants. Father shook his head in sadness. For the first time in all the years I'd known him, tears formed in his eyes. On Millie's chart, of course, blue ticket #4 was listed as a "groan," and #5 as "laughter," but on the chart I was keeping in my mind, here's how the discharges were listed:

Blue Ticket #4. Groan
   1. Visual function: golden light
   2. Emotional function: anger
Blue Ticket #5. Laughter
   1. Visual function: orange light
   2. Emotional function: disappointment
   3. Emotional function: sadness
   4. Cognitive function: certainty
   5. Optical function: microscopic vision
      a. Cells producing orange light
      b. Cells producing disappointment
      c. Cells producing sadness
      d. Cells producing certainty
   6. Optical Function: Father
      a. shaking head
      b. tears forming in his eyes

Mapping speech tissue was a bit more complex than mapping the Motor Strip. Once the rough outlines of the region had been defined by producing simple vocal response, Eli went back over it and mapped it more carefully, questioning me while the electrode was activated, to determine how much a particular cluster of cells had affected my language or comprehension. Counting was one of the easiest functions to test, and he used the same photographs we'd used with Lucinda to evaluate other functions like identification and word-retention.

If ever you want to explore the different ways a human being can make mistakes, you could certainly do worse than to put yourself up for neuro-stimulation. What I saw right away was that mistakes were not only a matter of what I said but what I thought I had said and how I felt about it. At blue ticket #4, for example, when I counted "One, two, three, five, four, six, eight," I was aware that I was wrong but the knowledge made no difference. In contrast, at #7 (less than .05 millimeter, I'd guess, posterior to #4), I counted wrong without realizing it, and at #9 and #10, I counted correctly but thought I hadn't. Also, there was more than one way to be wrong. At #8 and #11, I couldn't get beyond "one"; at #13, #15, and #16, I couldn't say a word; and at #14 (so close to #13 and #15 that I could barely distinguish them in the mirror), I said, "one, one, one, one, one" with the belief that each "one" was a progression beyond the one that had preceded it. In my mind, if not my voice, I was just on the verge of "six."

What was happening here, more than at any time since the craniotomy had begun, was a reversal of the roles normally played by what I took to be my brain and what I took to be myself. Sometimes, as at #4, it was clear that while "I" knew how to count correctly, "it" had caused me to do otherwise. Even as "I" counted incorrectly, "something in me" knew that I was doing so, and this "something" assumed control of my voice as soon as the electrode was deactivated. At times like these, I laughed or smiled at my mistake, crying "I knew it!" or slapping my palm against the table. No less frequent, however, were the times—#19 and #20—when "it" knew how to count but "I" counted incor-

rectly. As if a sort of will had intervened, as if "I" felt
compelled to make mistakes. Another thing I had not
expected was the different ways I treated my mistakes,
the different moods they could evoke. Sometimes (#4,
for example) a mistake embarassed me, sometimes (#9
and #10) it left me indifferent, and sometimes (#19 and
#20) it made me euphoric.

All of these different responses appeared as subheadings on the chart I was keeping for myself. Thus I found
that sadness was often followed at once by euphoria
and vice-versa; that disappointment could be long or
short-lived, serious or laughable. As for indifference, it
could be staunch and enduring, but sometimes too it
was easily weakened. One glance from Millie, who for
all her excitement and devotion could be brought to
the brink of tears by the sight of me babbling, could
make a tragedy out of an error I'd found, just an instant
before, totally insignificant.

Since the photographs required complex memories as
well as coordination between the visual and language
centers, the mistakes caused by the identification tests
were much more complicated than those produced by
counting. At #9 I called the house "a hosiery," and
then—when the electrode was deactivated—snapped
my fingers, crying, "Of course, it's a house!" Even after
that, however, "hosiery" lingered and "house," for all
the enthusiasm I'd brought to it, was unconvincing.
Sometimes I was mute when a photograph was shown,
but the muteness could be calm or hysterical. Much as
with counting, some mistakes left me indifferent, some

struck me as funny, and others seemed shameful, as if this bare instant of induced aphasia were an act of cowardice or stupidity or (at #22) an act of immorality, a violation of a taboo.

Sometimes, if I sensed a word just out of reach, my brain seemed to go into a spasm, as if every cell were grasping and sucking like an infant at the breast. On the other hand, if the word wasn't lurking, if a photograph left my mind a blank, my muteness could be pleasant, even revelatory, because the photograph ceased to be a photograph, and the object within it, liberated somehow by being unidentified, became more and more vivid, preternaturally real. For that instant there seemed to be nothing else but it in the world. Not only the operating room, not only Eli and Millie—I myself had disappeared within it. It was as if I'd gone on a voyage, and then, if the word suddenly appeared, as if I'd been brought home so quickly I couldn't get my bearings.

Words were like projectors that left the screen blank when they didn't appear or, when incorrect, cast images that were either out of focus or overexposed. Focus resumed when the electrode had been removed, awareness that made me correct myself, crying "tree!" or "house!" or "Of course, I was trying to say 'elephant'!" But as far as the focus itself was concerned, my feelings, as I say, were anything but unequivocal. I enjoyed "house" and "elephant," for example, but for reasons I could not discern, I found "tree" almost oppressive.

Sometimes, as with "umbrella," I had the word but couldn't bring it out. I thought "umbrella" but said "hat." Furthermore, "hat" immediately evoked synonyms—"cap" and "chapeau," for example, "helmet" and "headgear"—which, while I knew them to be incorrect, seemed to surround "umbrella" and make it less accessible. Photographs could also activate other circuits in my brain. When I saw a lemon I tasted it, and the taste produced the word, but when I was shown a baseball, I heard the crack of a bat, and then cried, not without conviction, "Hammer!" When Eli presented a schematic drawing of the sky, with stars and planets labelled, I heard several bars of "Silent Night," then saw Edward holding the doors of the elevator and could not stop the word: "Elevator!"

Not all my mistakes had logic, however. Some—like "rangid" and "wellentush," for a milk bottle and a kitten—were just babble, while others—like "airplane" for a television set—seemed intentional, perverse, or both. I also noted that some words came quickly and some took work. There were those that seemed to leap out of my brain the instant I saw the photograph and those I had to pause and think about, searching my memory for clues. In both cases I could get the right word in the end, but even if they sounded the same and were both listed on the chart as points that had not produced a language deficit, I knew very well that they were completely different. A word you looked for and a word that looked for you—how could you possibly think them the same?

At blue ticket #14, my right hand rose from the table and, unnoticed even by Martha, moved imperceptibly in the direction of my head. There was no doubt in my mind that the cells that produced this movement were located in the Motor Strip. One in particular was so highly charged that it flashed and received a constant stream of impulses, bombarding the cells adjacent to it while being bombarded by them in turn. How often we forget that neurons receive as well as transmit information! Cells like these were two-way systems that not only activated the muscles in my hand and arm but also received from other cells the various secretions that made their behavior "emotional" or "violent," "protective" or "destructive," with regard to the object toward which their movement was pointed. My hand dropped back to the table, but when it rose again—at what might have been blue ticket #19—I saw clearly that the movement was no longer a simple motor impulse. The cells in my brain that aimed at self-annihilation had seized control of it. I gasped.

"What is it?" Eli said.

"Rage and fear," I said. "I think it's time for the orange tickets."

Blue Ticket #18 had been placed just at the edge of the "Fissure of Sylvius," less than a millimeter away from a smaller convolution that looked like a question mark in reverse. Over the years, we'd come to use this latter fissure as a sort of landmark that separated language from "psychic" tissue. Since language tissue could often produce emotion and memory, while cells in this region frequently caused aphasia, the distinction was not precise, but it was sufficient for our purposes. We were surgeons, after all, not anatomists or physiologists. The mapping procedure and the localizations it demonstrated were not our primary interest. What we were after were the epileptic cells and the knowledge that we could remove them without causing language or motor deficits.

There were eleven orange labels before we reached the target tissue, and those points, like those involved with motor and language function, produced exactly the sort of behavior we'd learned to expect from them. Orange tickets #1 and #3 produced sexual sensations, great waves of desire and excitement which, at #5 and #6, were sufficient to cause an erection. At #4 I found myself, once again, in the elevator with Edward, listening to "Silent Night." The memory, as often in this region, was screened like a movie, terminating instantly when the electrode was deactivated, beginning again where it had before, when Eli stimulated the point again. Much as I had expected this sort of memory, often as I had produced it in patients of my own, Edward amazed me with his clarity and, most of all, his immediacy. It wasn't as if I remembered him but as if he were present. I could actually hear the music. The past had not completely displaced the present—I had not forgotten that I was on the operating table—but Edward's reality was so much more palpable than Eli's or Millie's that they seemed like apparitions beside him. He wasn't *remembered* and he certainly wasn't *imag-*

ined. Rather, it seemed as if he'd come alive in certain pockets of tissue that the rest of my brain, continuing in "the present," could not classify or describe.

When the first signs of seizure arose—at #9 and #10 this confusion of past and present continued in a slightly different form. Now the present seemed a memory, a re-living rather than a living. Like Edward, everything that happened—from the first stages of the seizure to the violent flailing that concluded it—was clearly remembered but, if anything, more real for being so. That is to say, everything, as I experienced it, had happened already. This distortion did not surprise me; *deja vu* is common during stimulation of the interpretive cortex, where circuits that secrete sensation are also connected to those that produce memory. Just as certain kinds of neurological short-circuits will lead one to believe that what is real is imagined and what's imagined real, it is inevitable, when circuits like these are involved, that what happens in the present will seem to be a memory, or for that matter, that what is remembered will seem to be unfolding in the moment.

How else explain the fact that when my seizure began I thought I was remembering it? That when my hand at last attacked my brain, I felt, not fear or sadness, but the calm and equanimity that one feels when— because his memory is functioning at its optimum level— all time seems circular and it is impossible to believe that anything is ever lost? In effect, I did not fear my death because it had already happened. Because it had left me alive to remember it.

We had always tried to avoid producing seizures on
the table, guiding ourselves with the electroencephalogram and edging a patient toward his epileptic
discharge without allowing it to gain control of him,
but not infrequently, as now, we went too far. Volatile
as it was, this tissue was indistinguishable, even under
a microscope, from the normal flesh that surrounded
it. Despite the fact that the epileptic focus was more or
less where we expected it to be, there was no way to
know how far it extended. "Something" told me, as Eli
placed the electrode at #11, that he might have gone
too far, but by then it was already too late to stop him,
even if I'd wanted to, because the circuits had already
been activated, and as we'd seen so many times with
seizures, once the discharge began, it spread as if in a
tidal wave to other regions of the brain.

The aura was worse than it had ever been, the odor
of feces filling the room and inducing an overwhelming
nausea. I doubt that more than thirty seconds elapsed
between its arrival and what I would experience as the
gentle, even joyous, union of my hand and brain, but
it seemed a long and leisurely voyage to me, a me-
thodical, systematic exploration of the whole neurological labyrinth. What made it especially wondrous was
that, through the magic of what, even then, I continued
to call my "hallucination," I observed the seizure's
progress as it moved across my cortex. With no less
clarity than I saw Millie's face beside the operating table
or Edward in the elevator, I saw one cell after another
receive, process, and transmit the excitation conveyed

to it, which had spread out in all directions from the epileptic focus. Only a fraction of an instant after excitation of the olfactory cells produced the noxious odor, I saw all that, saw it happen. And only a fraction of a second later, saw the impulse invade the auditory regions, the motor regions, spreading at last beyond the cortex to the mid-brain and finally the brain-stem itself, lifting perceptions and awareness to levels surpassing even those I'd known in earlier seizures, slowing time so that each of those thirty seconds seemed like hours and the seizure itself seemed to last a lifetime, enlarging my view of every neuron until, once again, I saw the particles of which it was composed. Screaming, grunting, arms and legs flailing, I saw pyrotechnical displays of flashing light, heard a screech so loud it pained my ears.

But nothing was disconnected from its source. I saw the agitation in my visual and auditory cells, the discharge that had caused me to grunt and scream, and when my arms contracted and my fingers grasped at the soft grey tissue I saw in the mirror, I saw the motor neurons in which the contraction and grasping originated.

Millie screamed and Eli grabbed for my hand, but not quickly enough to stop me. The flesh was gelatinous, warmer somehow than I'd expected, so slippery and resilient that I could barely get hold of it. I felt the tickets we had placed, and I felt the midcerebral artery on which my eyes had been fixed since the first moments of the craniotomy. It was surprisingly tough and fibrous, but it collapsed as if deflating once I got it between my fingertips. Blood filled the mirror when it punctured. As I've noted, whether from *deja vu* or because hallucinations similar to these had occurred during previous seizures, none of this was new; all of it had happened before, all was duplication. The only difference was the clarity with which I saw it.

Thus a lifetime of blindness ended. For once I had no filters on my eyes. I saw the neurons that caused my arms and legs to flail, the tiny explosions in the auditory regions that generated all this screeching in my ears, the cells that produced the distortion we called "the *deja vu* response," and more vividly than any others, the cells in my Optic Lobe that made such vision possible. Discharging with rapid and rhythmic frequency, they fed my vision with sharper images, greater magnifications, until finally it seemed that my eyes had burrowed into the depths of space, casting off the fear and resistance that had kept their view on the surface of things and restricted it to fractions of the world.

Millions, billions, trillions of times enlarged, my neurons dissolved into fragments, and then each fragment dissolved into the particles of which it was composed. Between any two neurons the expanse that loomed was vast as the universe. Finally, by the grace of its own perception, my brain was an infinity of flux that only the most accurate brain-damaged vision could hope to comprehend. Watching the protoplasm within the cells that pulled my hand in their direction, the particles within that protoplasm that generated terror, the elec-

trons and protons within the particles that produced
the word for terror—"bliss"—I saw them all, at last, as
empty space and understood, at last, that there was
nothing there for my hand to grasp.

"Have you seen enough?" Eli said.

"Yes," I said, meaning "no."